MATHEMATICAL MAGIC

William Simon

PREFACE BY
MARTIN GARDNER

DOVER PUBLICATIONS, INC.
New York

Dedicated to my lovely wife Rona,
who is more bewildered
when my mathematical magic doesn't work
than when it does!

Published in Canada by General Publishing Company, Ltd., 30 Lesmill Road, Don Mills, Toronto, Ontario.
Published in the United Kingdom by Constable and Company, Ltd., 3 The Lanchesters, 162–164 Fulham Palace Road, London W6 9ER.

This Dover edition, first published in 1993, is an unabridged, unaltered republication of the work first published by Charles Scribner's Sons ("The Scribner Library"—"Emblem Editions"), New York, 1964. Martin Gardner has written a Preface specially for the Dover edition, and one minor typographical error has been corrected.

Manufactured in the United States of America
Dover Publications, Inc., 31 East 2nd Street, Mineola, N.Y. 11501

Library of Congress Cataloging-in-Publication Data

Simon, William, 1927–1988.
Mathematical magic / William Simon ; preface by Martin Gardner.
p. cm.
Originally published: New York : Scribner, 1964.
Includes index.
ISBN 0-486-27593-0 (pbk.)
1. Mathematical recreations. 2. Conjuring. I. Title.
QA95.S495 1993
793.7′4—dc20 93-15007
CIP

preface

William Simon (1927–1988) was one of the nation's most skillful and creative card magicians. Professionally he was a businessman, president of a firm in New Jersey that made brake blocks for cars. I suspect that Bill loved magic much more than brake blocks. He was the inventor of scores of subtle card "moves," as magicians like to call them. Most of them are described in Bill's technical books sold only to the magic fraternity: *Controlled Miracles* (1949), *Effective Card Magic* (1952), and *Sleightly Sensational* (1954). Many of his original tricks appeared in a magic journal called *The Phoenix*.

Mathematical Magic is a nontechnical collection of easy-to-do, self-working tricks based on mathematical principles. My *Mathematics, Magic and Mystery* (another Dover book)* was the first to range widely over this curious field. Bill's book was the second. Hundreds of strange mathematical tricks have been invented since, but Bill's book is as good an introduction as any to this fascinating hybrid field that is half conjuring and half mathematics.

I had the privilege of knowing Bill as a good friend. He introduced me to my present (and only) wife on a blind date that I remember fondly. He was best man at my wedding in Manhattan, performed without charge by our friend Judge Starke, another amateur magician. I always relished Bill's great sense of humor—he could have

*[Published 1956; still available from Dover, ISBN 0-486-20335-2.]

been a successful stand-up comic—especially at sessions with our mutual friend Bob Orben, the celebrated jokesmith, and speech writer for President Gerald Ford.

Bill died tragically of Alzheimer's disease at the early age of 61. He left notebooks crammed with card ideas. Unfortunately only he could interpret them.

MARTIN GARDNER

contents

foreword

One of the most enjoyable aspects of *Mathematical Magic* is that you need not be a magician or a mathematician to be able to enjoy, understand, and actually demonstrate the various principles and stunts described in this book.

Using mathematics as a base, various tricks and effects have been developed that are entertaining yet require little more than your knowledge of the working principle. If you can add simple figures together you can handle the tricks. If you can remember the proper sequence of steps, as clearly described in the text, you will have no difficulty demonstrating many fascinating problems and magical effects to your friends. The word "problems" is perhaps ill-advised, as this is not a puzzle book . . . the only problem you will create is "How did you do that!"

The mathematician or magician should find several interesting items directly or indirectly related to his specific field. To the uninitiated, however, a most marvelous field of mathematical principles will soon parade before his eyes. And these principles have been applied to tricks-stunts-effects as a means of giving him a vehicle for using and understanding many useful mathematical ways and means.

Mathematics pre-dates recorded history, and so it is extremely difficult to credit to all the originators material discussed in this book. I have attempted to credit all items which I could identify. Thus, if any oversights have been made, they were unintentional.

I do wish to specifically thank the clever writer-mathematician-magician Mr. Martin Gardner for his valued advice and encouragement. And for those interested in *Mathematical Magic,* I might suggest their perusal of Mr. Gardner's various books on allied fields, or his monthly column on advanced mathematics and theory, which is published in "Scientific American."

To my wife Rona I extend my deepest appreciation for her assistance in helping me complete this book.

One final word of advice, and this is directed to those who will use the items discussed in this book: Be sure to run through the items you plan to use so that you can demonstrate them with certainty, with complete understanding, and in an entertaining manner. You will then be sure of performing real *mathematical magic!*

August 25, 1963 WILLIAM SIMON

MATHEMATICAL MAGIC

Chapter 1

magic with numbers

Mathematics has given form and order to our sciences of the past, the present, and it has set the groundwork for the future. From the movements of our watches to the symbols on the work-pad of a nuclear physicist, from waking to sleeping, we are dependent upon mathematics and its endless applications.

Of course, mathematics is not merely the science of numbers. It is concerned with many fields such as topology (the mathematics of shape), cybernetics (thinking machines), algebra, geometry, and many other schools.

The fascinating lure is not only the tremendous amount of development that has already been completed, but the exciting new discoveries that are constantly being uncovered. New fields to explore, new uses and applications of these wondrous tools, imaginative theories and possibilities beyond the ken of the average person.

In addition to these practical, somber, and intellectual values, mathematics has its appealing recreational aspects. Many principles can be applied in amusing ways. Strange coincidences occur. Unexpected relationships can be uncovered. Applying these principles in amusing ways, actively or passively, can bring much personal enjoyment. You may wish to show these "curiosities" as stunts or tricks for your friends, or you may choose simply to enjoy them for their own sake. Regardless of how you plan to use this "less serious side of mathematics," you are assured of much fun.

Mathematical Magic is the end result of my interest in recreational mathematics. You will find suggestions on presentations of several of the items so that you will have a picture as to the manner in which you may show these curiosities. For the most part, they should be presented as tricks, or stunts, or unusual phenomena. Attitudes of this sort will cloak many of the principles, and in addition, lend credence to procedures which would in other instances be questioned.

Arithmetic—the magic of numbers—will be our first concern. Elementary principles can be quite interesting . . . if properly handled. For example, it is possible to utilize an obvious relationship between numbers to render surprising results . . . provided that you take the necessary steps to cloak the obvious. This first item deals with just such a situation.

(1) the multi-player

If we divide a number by another number the result can be multiplied by the divisor to return to the dividend (original number which was divided). For example, if we divide 2 into 10 the result is 5. By multiplying the result (5) by the divisor (2), we return to the original dividend: 10 (5 × 2 equals 10).

By expanding a relationship such as this we can build an interesting "experiment." To conceal the obvious it is necessary to use numbers which are too cumbersome for simple mental computations. By using the number 12,345,679 it is possible to multiply this number to result in a product of 111,111,111 or 222,222,222 or 333,333,333 or on up to 999,999,999. Restated, by using certain multipliers it is possible to control the product (result) of multiplying 12,345,679 so that the product will be a nine place number ranging from 111,111,111 to 999,999,999 with all digits being the same value.

The number 12,345,679 is not a chance selection. It was arrived at by dividing 9 into 111,111,111. You will find this division to result in the answer: 12,345,679. Now, if you multiply 12,345,679 by 9 it will of course revert back to the original dividend: 111,111,111. This reciprocity is the same relationship as that cited using the dividend 10 and dividing it by 2. The main difference is that the relationship is obvious with the number 10 whereas it is obscured when using an eight place number such as 12,345,679.

Using 12,345,679; the "key" number is 9. We know that using 9 as the multiplier will result in the product 111,111,111. By doubling 9 (2 × 9) and using 18 as the multiplier the product will be 222,222,222. By tripling 9 (3 × 9) and using 27 as the multiplier of 12,345,679 the product will be 333,333,333. In fact, multiplying *any* digit by 9, and using the number arrived at as the multiplier of 12,345,679 will result in a nine digit answer, with all digits being the number multiplied by 9. Although the digit 8 doesn't appear in the number 12,345,679 the principle still applies: Using 72 (8 × 9) as the multiplier will result in the product 888,888,888.

As you can see, you can control the result by using the proper multiplier. Other combinations may be easily developed if you wish to use this principle with other numbers. For example, the number 15,873 may be used in a manner similar to that as shown above. But the "key" number changes. Using the number 15,873 requires that 7 be used as the "key." If you multiply 15,873 by 7 the result will be 111,111. If 15,873 is multiplied by 14 (2 × 7) the result will be 222,222. If multiplied by 63 (9 × 7) the result will be 999,999. Thus, a similar relationship exists. Of course, 15,873 is found by dividing 7 into 111,111. As suggested above, with a little experimentation you can develop other unusual combinations should you desire to pursue this further.

Returning to 12,345,679; to use this as a stunt it is necessary to introduce this number to your spectators in a way which will be acceptable to them. To do this, begin by discussing the tremendous problem the telephone company has in making and recording the many telephone listings which any major city, county, or state requires. "An engineer for the telephone company recently discovered that New York City has twelve million, three hundred and forty-five thousand, six hundred and seventy-nine separate listings of individuals, places of business, and yellow page listings," you would say.

Continue as follows: "The interesting thing about this number of listings is that the number itself has unusual possibilities. Let me show you. Please write down the number twelve million, three hundred and forty-five thousand, six hundred and seventy-nine on a piece of paper. This is the number of listings."

Assuming this has been done correctly your spectator will write 12,345,679: and you will have introduced the number in an innocent manner. Ask your spectator to "Please pass the pencil over this number, and whenever you feel an impulse I want you to draw a circle around the digit at that point. In other words, freely choose one of the digits."

Let us assume that your spectator has circled the digit 5. You mentally multiply this by the "key" number 9 (9 × 5 equals 45) and immediately introduce the number by saying, "There are 45 main relay points in the New York City telephone circuit. Would you please multiply the number of listings (12,345,679) by 45."

If your instructions have been followed correctly the following will appear on the paper:

```
 12,34(5),679
        × 45
 ------------
    61728395
   49382716
 ------------
 555,555,555
```

Your concluding remarks could well be, "Isn't that a strange coincidence, the very number you circled! And do you know, if you were to dial 555,555,555 I guarantee that you will always get . . . a busy signal!"

Of course, you always multiply the selected digit by 9 (your "key" number) and introduce this product as the multiplier. If, as may occasionally happen, your spectator mentions that 8 doesn't appear and he would like to circle the number 8, you proceed by having him use 72 (8×9) as the multiplier. As mentioned earlier, the principle will apply to any digit.

(2) a matter of age

Over the centuries the number 9 has gained a reputation for having mysterious properties. Its use, in various arithmetical computations, seems to present it with a magic halo. Actually, as the late puzzle genius Sam Lloyd, Senior, pointed out; the number 9 is not imbued with supernatural characteristics . . . it is its position as the last single digit in our numerical system which lends itself to many flexible uses. If our system was built on 5 digits, for example, then the number 5 would inherit these characteristics.

I mention this because 9 is an extremely convenient and popularly used number. The following item uses the number 9 as a "key" number, but I will discuss how other numbers may be used if you wish.

An amusing sequence is one in which you determine a person's age although you are given very limited information. There are many systems for doing this, but the method described here is not, to my knowledge, too well known.

Have a spectator (whose age you couldn't possibly know) assist you. He is to perform the following operations while you are turned away from him so that you can't see what he writes:

(a) He is to write his age on a slip of paper. (Let us assume that he is 34 years old and thus writes "34" on the paper.)

(b) He is to write "your lucky number" beneath his age. Inform him that your lucky number is 90. Thus, he writes 90 beneath his age.

(c) He is to add these two numbers together. If this has been done correctly, it will appear as follows:

$$\begin{array}{r} 34 \\ 90 \\ \hline 124 \end{array}$$

(d) He is now instructed to cross out the digit to the left of his total and transplant "whatever this digit is" beneath the remaining numbers in the total. He lastly adds the transplanted number to the number directly above it. If your instructions have been performed correctly, things should appear as follows:

$$\begin{array}{r} 34 \\ 90 \\ \hline \not{1}24 \\ 1 \\ \hline 25 \end{array}$$

(e) At this point you mention that your spectator has arrived at a total which has no relation to his age, or to any of the numbers worked with. You request that he tell you what this number is. He will tell you that the total is 25. On the basis of this information you are able to tell the spectator his age! Of course, this should be disclosed in an impressive manner.

(f) Your work is quite simple. Upon learning the total (in this case it is 25) you simply add 9 to it. This will give you the spectator's age (25 plus 9 equals 34).

At this point I suggest that you try the above with your own age, or with any two digit number. Follow the indicated steps and add 9 to the total arrived at in step "e." You will return to your age (or the number you started with).

The working behind this is quite novel. At one point you have 90 added in (step "b"), and at another point you have 99 taken away (step "d" actually results in a reduction of 99 from the total). The net result is a subtraction of 9 from your spectator's original starting number . . . his age. Thus, when you are told the final total, you need merely add 9 to it to bring it back to its original value.

As mentioned, 9 is a convenient number to use in this stunt. This can be changed simply by changing the number you have the spectator add to his age. For example, if 85 was "your lucky number" and you had spectator add 85 to his age (in step "b") instead of 90, then to find spectator's age you would have to add 14 to the total given to you (instead of 9).

As an illustration, using 34 as spectator's age, add 85 to it (34 plus 85 equals 119). The digit to the left, 1, is crossed out and then added to the remaining digits (1 plus 19 equals 20). Thus, you would be given the total 20. To this add 14 (secretly) and you return to the original age 34 (20 plus 14).

Any "lucky number" may be used providing that this number *and* your spectator's age will total over 100. You simply subtract your "lucky number" from 99 to determine what number you must secretly add to the final total given to you to return the number to its original value. For example, if you choose to have your spectator use 77 as your "lucky number" you would secretly add 22 to the final total (77 subtracted from 99). To illustrate, let us assume that your spectator is 34 and he adds "your lucky number" 77 to his age.

The total would be 111 (77 plus 34). He would then be instructed to cross out the digit to the left (a 1), and transpose this beneath the remaining digits. The remaining digits (11) would be added to the transposed digit (11 plus 1) and you would be given the total 12. To this you secretly add 22, which would bring you back to your spectator's age: 34 (12 plus 22).

In showing this to your friends it is important that your spectator clearly understands your instructions. This can be an amusing parlor stunt, and you can vary the "lucky number" as you wish.

The next item, The Fibonacci Series, is quite novel and uses an interesting and little used principle.

(3) the fibonacci series

Adding numbers in a series is an unusual procedure. A Fiboncacci Series is a series of numbers added in an uncommon fashion. To explain a Fibonacci Series, and develop it into an amusing trick, the following will describe what your spectators would see:

(a) A slip of paper is handed to your spectators, with a row of numbers listed 1 through 10 appearing on the slip.

(b) Explaining that they are going to freely choose numbers which you do not wish to see, you stand in a position so that you can't see what is written on the paper. The first spectator is requested to write any number he chooses alongside of the first position on the paper.

(c) The second spectator is also requested to freely select a number and write this beneath the first number. (This would place second spectator's number in the second position.)

(d) These two numbers are added together by the spectators, and the total is placed in the third position.

(e) The two last numbers (the numbers in the second and third position) are now added together, and their total is placed in the fourth position.

(f) This process, of adding the last two numbers, is carried on until all positions (10) have been filled. (This procedure, of adding the last two numbers together in a series, is known as a Fibonacci Series.)

(g) At this point the spectators are requested to total the 10 numbers. Before they complete the addition of the ten numbers you announce the total!

This can be a most surprising conclusion. Freely chosen numbers are selected at the start of the "series," no stooges, and you have a minimum of work to do to perform this stunt.

The method is based upon the fact that numbers added in a series of this nature have a relationship. Stated simply, the succeeding numbers are fractional components of preceding numbers. The number in the seventh position is actually 1/11th of the *final* total of the ten numbers. Thus, if you can secretly learn the value of the seventh number you need merely to multiply this by 11 to know the total of the ten numbers. Knowing what the seventh number is, even before your spectators have filled in the eighth, ninth, or tenth positions gives you a tremendous advantage in adding to the effectiveness of this principle.

I will discuss ways for you to secure the necessary information (without arousing undue suspicions), several interesting ways to bring the effect to a climax, and a simple system for multiplying any number by 11 (so that you can make a quick, mental calculation).

First, the effect. Let us assume that the first spectator chooses the number 27 and the second spectator selects the number 8, and they proceed with the addition process as described above. If they have followed your instructions correctly, they will have written the following:

1.	27
2.	8
3.	35
4.	43
5.	78
6.	121
7.	199
8.	320
9.	519
10.	839
	2189

Of course, the number in the third position (in this instance, 35) is the total of 27 and 8. The number in the fourth position (43) is the total of 8 and 35. Note that the number in the seventh position (199), when multiplied by 11, will result in a product of 2189—and this is the exact sum of the ten numbers.

You must learn the seventh number, and as suggested above, it is best to do this before your spectators have completed filling in the ten positions. A simple way to do this is to have your spectators start filling in the various numbers. Work your way towards them, and when you estimate that they should be up to the seventh position simply turn to them and say: "Are you doing this correctly?" and as you ask this, glance at the paper and spot the number in the seventh position. Then turn back immediately. (I've used this simple ruse many times, and have never been called on this.) Assuming that your spectators haven't completed the seventh position, then they probably have finished the sixth number. In this case you would simply note the numbers in the fifth and sixth positions, and mentally add them together to give you the number in the seventh position.

Once you have determined the seventh number you multiply it by 11. This computation should be completed while your spectators are still filling in the ten positions. After your spectators have filled in the ten positions request that they add all ten numbers together. Point out that freely selected numbers were chosen, that they were added together in an unusual fashion, and that you couldn't possibly know the total.

While your spectators are performing the addition you state, "Before I started to show this to you a number kept coming into my mind. It just kept appearing before me—2189, 2189, 2189. What is your total?" Of course, when your spectators arrive at their total you will have a surprising conclusion.

Other ways of bringing this effect to a conclusion are as follows:

(a) After you have learned the necessary information (and have multiplied by 11) have your spectators add the ten numbers. Request that they "concentrate on this freely arrived-at total." After simulated mental effort you read their minds by slowly announcing the total "which they are thinking of."

(b) Upon completing your computation quickly write the total (11 times the seventh number) on a slip of paper and hand this to one of the spectators saying, "Please hold this until after you've added the numbers together." Of course, your computation should have been finished before your spectators start the addition. When they have completed adding the ten numbers, you will receive credit for predicting the total after they open the slip of paper and see that your inscription is identical to the total.

(c) This presentation eliminates the necessity of glimpsing the seventh number, and it may also earn you a reputation for being a "lightning calculator." Have your spectators fill in the ten positions while you are in another room or situated so that you can't possibly see any of their writings. After they have finished you say, "I've developed a photographic memory and an adding machine brain. I am going to ask you to hold the ten numbers in front of me for one second, ten numbers arrived at in a completely free manner. In that one second I will attempt to memorize the ten numbers. I will then try to add them together and arrive at a total quicker than the both of you working together with pencil and paper." Have the spectators put the paper in front of you. Quickly note the seventh number, and once you've got it turn away from the paper. Request that they add the ten numbers together. You immediately multiply by 11. As soon as you complete the computation you announce your total. This should be long before your spectators complete their addition of the ten numbers.

The following is a short-cut method to multiply any number by 11. Let us use the number 199 in this illustration as this was the number in the seventh position in the above description of the Fibonacci Series. With the number 199 in your mind, mentally place a letter above each digit as follows:

abc
199

To build the total, your first step is to place the "c" number to the right in your mental answer. Thus, the digit which will be the unit digit in your mental answer is 9. Next, add "c" and "b" together (9 plus 9 equals 18) and place the 8 next to the 9 in your mental answer (to the left of it—in the tens column) carrying the 1 left over. Your mental answer at this point will be 89.

Add "b" and "a" together, plus the 1 you carried over (9 plus 1 plus 1 equals 11). Place the digit 1 in your mental answer, carrying over 1. Your mental answer will now be 189. Add the carried over digit, 1, to "a" (1 plus 1 equals 2) and place this alongside of the 189 in your mental answer. Thus, you will have arrived at the product 2189, which is 11 times 199.

You will note the simple pattern used to perform this computation. As another example, let us multiply 758429 by 11.

(a) Place the 9 (unit digit) to the right in your mental answer.

(b) Add 9 plus 2 (11) and place the right hand digit alongside the 9 in your mental answer, carrying over 1. Mental answer at this point is 19.

(c) Add 2 plus 4 plus 1 (the carry over), and place this total (7) in your mental answer. Note that there is no carry over in this instance. Mental answer at this point is 719.

(d) Add 4 plus 8 (12) and place the 2 in your answer, carrying over 1. Mental answer at this point is 2719.

(e) Add 8 plus 5 plus 1 (the carry over) for a total of 14, and place the 4 in your answer, carrying over the 1. Mental answer at this point is 42719.

(f) Add 5 plus 7 plus 1 (carry over) for a total of 13, and place the 3 in your answer, carrying over the 1. Mental answer at this point is 342719.

(g) To the last number, 7, add the carry over 1 and place this total of 8 in your answer. At this point the correct product will have been attained: 8342719.

This system of multiplication by 11 is very useful when showing the Fibonacci Series effect to your friends as the number in the seventh position is usually a three or four digit number, and this is quite easy to handle mentally.

(4) finding a number

An interesting and little known problem is to find a digit which has been "lost." Let us assume that your spectator selects a four or five place number (a random selection). You then request that he "lose" one of the digits by simply drawing a line through it. After a few simple computations you name the "lost" digit even though you had no knowledge of the original number used and did not see any of the computations!

Here are the mechanics:

(a) A spectator writes down any number he wishes. He does this while you are out of the room or in a position so that you could not possibly see what he writes. (Note: Any multi-digit number may be used, but a four or five place number will take less time than a larger number and is thus more desirable.) Let us assume that your spectator chooses the number 7438 at random and writes this on a slip of paper.

(b) Request that he add together the digits which comprise the number he has chosen. "Add the digits together by adding the first to the second, this total to the third digit, and this total to the fourth. For example, if you chose the number 1234 you would add them to a total of 10 . . . 1 plus 2 plus 3 plus 4." If your spectator adds his digits together correctly (7438) he will arrive at a total of 22. Have this total placed to the right of the number he originally selected.

(c) Request that he "lose" one of the digits from his original number by drawing a line through it. He may "lose" whichever digit he desires. Let us assume that he draws a line through the 4.

(d) Have him place the remaining three-digit number (in this case, 738) directly above the number he placed to the right (22), and he is requested to subtract the smaller number from the larger. If your instructions have been carried out correctly then your spectator will have written the following:

$$7\not{4}38 \qquad \begin{array}{r} 738 \\ -\ 22 \\ \hline 716 \end{array}$$

(e) You now say, "You have arrived at a number which I couldn't possibly know and which has no relation to either your originally selected number or to the "lost" number. What is that number?" In this example, your spectator will tell you that the number he has arrived at is 716. Using this number, you are able to discover the "lost" number!

(f) Upon learning the number, add the digits together to bring it down to a single digit. Using 716, you add 7 plus 1 plus 6 for a total of 14. You then add 1 plus 4 (the remaining digits) for a total of 5. (This is known as casting out the nines, and this will be discussed in greater detail.) To find the "lost" digit you simply subtract 5 from 9. This would leave 4, and thus you know that 4 was the "lost" digit. Reveal this in a dramatic fashion to add to the effect. *Note:* 9 is always used to subtract from in performing this stunt.

Another example of this in action: Let us assume that the spectator has chosen the number 85129, which he secretly writes on the paper. He adds the five digits together (8 plus 5 plus 1 plus 2 plus 9) for a total of 25, and writes 25 alongside of the original five digit number. Let us assume that he draws a line ("loses") the 8. Thus, he writes the remaining four digit number, 5129, over 25 and proceeds to subtract 25 from this number. The result of this subtraction, 5104, is mentioned to you. You add the digits together (5 plus 1 plus 0 plus 4) for a total of 10, and bring this down to a single digit (1 plus 0), which is 1. Upon subtracting 1 from 9 your result, 8, is the "lost" digit.

When you are told the number spectator has arrived at, if you should find that it is a 9 after reducing it to a single digit, then the "lost" digit was either a 0 or a 9.

Regarding casting out the nines, when a number is reduced to a single digit we are actually "casting out" or removing all nines and reducing the number to its simplest state *minus* all nines and multiples of nine. For example, in a simple number such as 10, when we add the digits together (1 plus 0) we reduce this to the single digit 1. We have actually cast out a 9. Using the number 30, for example, we bring this down to the single digit 3 (3 plus 0). 3 is actually 30 with three 9's cast out (three 9's equal 27, 27 plus 3 equals 30). This works exactly as above with multi-digit numbers of any size.

Using the number 7438, if we were to add the digits together (22) and subtract 22 from 7438 the remainder would be a multiple of 9, and this multiple—when reduced to a single digit—will be 9. (22 subtracted from 7438 leaves a remainder of 7416. Reducing this to a single digit (7 plus 4 plus 1 plus 6 equals 18, 1 plus 8 equals 9) results in 9. The mechanics behind this is that the total of the digits, 22, is actually the number 7438 with the 9's cast out. Actually, 22 can be further reduced to 4 (2 plus 2). Note that subtracting 4 from 7438 leaves a remainder of 7434, and this, upon being reduced to a single digit number, arrives at the number 9.

The above applies to all numbers. For example, using 85129 and adding the digits together (25 . . . which can further be reduced to 7 by adding the 2 and the 5 together), we will arrive at a multiple of 9 by subtracting 25 from 85129 (and also by subtracting 7 from 85129). 25 from 85129 leaves 85104. Adding these digits together results in 9 when reducing them to a single digit.

In performing the "lost" number we do not subtract the cast out number from the *original* number, we actually subtract the cast out number from a number with a missing digit. Using 7438, we subtracted the sum of the digits (22) from the number 738 (since the digit 4 in the number was "lost"). Thus, we arrived at a remainder which, upon being reduced to a single digit, was the difference between the "lost" digit and 9. Note: If we subtract 18 from 738 (18 is the sum of the digits 7 plus 3 plus 8) the remainder is 720. And 720, upon being reduced to a single digit, becomes 9. This should give you a clear explanation of the working of the "lost" digit effect.

Casting out the 9's can be used in many ways. One practical application is that used by accountants to check figures on multiplication. Let us assume that you had to multiply 74361 by 83488. The correct product of this multiplication is 6,208,251,168. A quick way of checking the accuracy of this is to cast out the 9's. First, cast out the 9's of the multiplier and the multiplicand. (83488 is reduced to the single digit 4, and 74361 is brought down to the digit 3.) Multiply these two digits (4 × 3 equals 12) and bring the product down to a single digit

(12: 1 plus 2 equals 3). Thus, with the 9's cast out, the product of this multiplication is 3. Now reduce the product of the major number to a single digit: 6 plus 2 plus 0 plus 8 plus 2 etc. You will find that with the 9's cast out the product comes down to 3! With this agreement, you can be reasonably sure that the computation is correct. Of course, there can be an error even when using this as a check, but if there is an error (with the numbers agreeing) then the error is either a 9 or a multiple of 9.

As mentioned earlier, the number 9 does not have mysterious properties. If our system was based on 7 digits instead of 9 then the number 7 would develop these unusual characteristics. Of course, in such a system we could not express numbers in the same fashion as that which we now use. The number 17, in a seven digit system, would indicate 15 (8 plus 7). 27 would indicate 23 (8 plus 8 plus 7). I mention this so that if you apply the above principles to numbers other than 9 you must correctly express and interpret the numbers you use.

One final use of casting out the 9's: An interesting "age divination" stunt may be performed. Have a spectator write any number he wishes on a piece of paper. Have him multiply this number by 9. Have him add his age to this product. After he has completed these operations request that he name the final total. On the basis of this number you correctly "divine" the spectator's age. Of course, you should point out that you couldn't know his age, nor the number he selected. And the number he chooses can be any size.

Let us assume that the spectator selects the number 17819. After he has secretly multiplied this by 9 he will arrive at the product 160,371. Let us also assume that your spectator is 33 years old. Thus, he adds 33 to the above product for a total of 160,404. The total he mentions to you is 160,404.

Upon learning this number you immediately cast out the nines, bringing it down to a two-digit number, or one-digit if you wish. In this case 160,404 is brought down to 15 (1 plus 6 plus 0 plus 4 plus 0 plus 4). You now know that your spectators age is a multiple of 9 *plus* 15. (If you had brought his total down to a single digit then his age would have been a multiple of 9 *plus* 6.)

Using a bit of judgement you simply add 9 to the number you have arrived at, in this case you would add 9 to 15 for a total of 24. Your spectator will certainly appear older than 24, so to 24 you add another 9 which brings you to a total of 33. Of course, your spectator will appear to be this age, so you confidently announce his age as 33. Assuming that you are in doubt, you could mentally add another 9 to 33, for a total of 42, but in this case by the appearance of your spectator you should know that he isn't 42, so simply revert back to 33.

The working of this is quite simple. Let us assume that your spectator selected the number 1111. Upon multiplying this by 9 his product would be 9999. Assuming that he is 33 years old, upon adding this to 9999 the total arrived at will be 10,032. Upon learning this total you cast out the nines, which brings it down to 6. You begin adding 9's to the 6 until you arrive at a total which you can safely estimate as the correct age. Of course, in this case you build up to 33 and announce this as your spectator's age. You must judge to within 9 years of your spectator's age to do this stunt, and this should offer very little difficulty.

In essence, when you multiply by 9 and then cast out nines you are simply cancelling out the number spectator has freely selected. Since he has added his age to this number, your result is actually the elimination of the freely chosen number and the casting out of the nines of his age! Once you have reduced to the single digit, you then build it back up again (adding in 9's) until you return to his age.

As a final example of this, let us assume that your spectator is 47 years old and the number he secretly selects is 75481. Upon multiplying 75481 by 9 your spectator will arrive at the product 679,329; and upon adding 47 to this he will arrive at the total 679,376. Casting the nines out of this number will bring you to the two-digit number 38. Using judgement, you determine that he appears older than 38, thus you add 9 to 38 for a total of 47. This should appear to be his correct age, and you announce it as such. But if you are in doubt, you can add another 9 to it for a total of 56. Of course, this is done mentally, and it should be obvious to you that your spectator is not this old, so you revert back to 47.

Once you understand the principles the methods will appear to you to be quite obvious, but you will be surprised how deceptive these will appear on showing them to your friends.

(5) the cycloid

A cycloid* is a number which repeats itself endlessly. For example, if we were to divide 7 into 1, the answer would be .142857142857142857 etc. A never ending cycle of the number 142857 constantly repeated. This particular cycloid, 142857, has interesting characteristics.

If 142857 is multiplied by an digit from 2 to 6 the product of this will be a six-digit number that consists of the cycloid numbers. Below you will find the products of multiplying 142857 by these various digits:

2 × 142857 equals 285714
3 × 142857 equals 428571
4 × 142857 equals 571428
5 × 142857 equals 714285
6 × 142857 equals 857142

Note that if 142857 was strung together in a band or circle this circle could be broken at any point to show the correct product of multiplication by the above digits. The numbers continue to run in proper sequence, but at different "starting" points.

* Technically, this is actually a cyclical number. A cycloid has other characteristics.

There are limited practical applications of this, but I have developed an amusing prediction stunt that you can perform with this cycloid. You will require a few items to show this, but the results are well worth the effort in securing the necessary "props."

You will require a piece of chalk, a small piece of slate material 3″ × 5″ (a piece of tough black cardboard will do), pencil, and paper. Also, on the reverse side of one of your business cards (or a blank card) write:

Professor Future—Telephone No. 142857

(With the advent of multi-digit phone numbers this will be accepted as an up-dated telephone listing.)

Begin by discussing how it is possible for some people to predict the future. The Rhine E.S.P. experiments could be mentioned. Then say, "I know a mindreader who professionally works under the name of Professor Future. He left his phone number with me so that I could contact him if I could use his services for a show. (Bring out the card which bears the number as discussed above.) He even taught me an experiment that I can demonstrate to show you that it is possible to predict the future. I will attempt this for two reasons . . . first of all, you look skeptical. Second of all, I planned it this way!"

Remove the chalk and slate from your pocket and have these objects examined. State that you are going to write a prediction on the slate.

Pick up the slate and write the number 4285714285.
Keep the slate towards your body so that your spectators can't see what you have written. Place the slate, writing downwards, on a table. Remark that you have made a prediction about an event that hasn't even taken place yet, something that no one could possibly anticipate. (Note: Instead of memorizing the ten-place number you can pencil this number on the bottom of the slate in very light lettering. This will go unnoticed by your spectators, and will relieve you of any memory work.)

"To continue," you say, "we require a number, any number. Let's use Professor Future's telephone number. Since he is a man of unusual powers it may have magical possibilities." Have your spectator write 142857 on the piece of paper.

"I want you to multiply this by a freely chosen number. To save time, please select any number from, say, one to six. This will give you a good range and not involve difficult multiplication." Your spectators should offer little resistance to this suggestion.

Let us assume that your spectator chooses 5 as the multiplier. As soon as he starts to perform the multiplication of 142857 by 5 you perform the following simple task: you multiply the digit of his choice by 7. Since 7 is the last number in 142857 it will be the first number *he* will multiply. The answer, in this case, is 35 (7 × 5). Thus, you have learned that the number 5 will be the unit digit in the product (the last digit in the answer).

You know that 5 will be the right hand digit in your spectator's product. You must now secretly erase four excessive digits which appear on the slate . . . and you must do this without arousing any suspicions.

To do this casually pick up the slate, as shown here:

Note that the writing is towards your body, and that your fingers are towards the back of the slate and your thumbs are on the face of the slate: near your chalked prediction.

In this case you know that 5 is the right hand digit in the answer, thus, you must erase the four digits (4285) which are nearest your left thumb. You do this by simply rubbing your left thumb over these digits. As you do this (and don't glance at the slate during the erasure) you say, "Please don't make any mistakes in your multiplication." As soon as you've completed the necessary erasures replace the slate. The entire operation should take a few seconds and it will appear that you have simply picked up the slate for a moment and then replaced it. Your spectator should still be working on his computation. After you have replaced the slate walk several feet away from it.

After your spectator has completed his multiplication I suggest that you build up to a climax. Call to your spectator's attention the fact that you wrote a prediction *before* anything was done. This is a very strong point, so make the most of it. Point out that your spectator freely chose a number to use as a multiplier, and thus a product was arrived at that couldn't have been known or controlled. Finally, dramatically show that your prediction correctly foretold the result! The following diagram shows your prediction as it will appear:

It may be necessary to make erasures with both thumbs. This should offer little problem as you need merely move your right thumb to the left (eliminating whatever numbers are unnecessary) or your left thumb to the right. The body of six numbers always stays together. It is simply four of the "fringe" numbers which must be erased.

To review briefly, after your spectator has selected a digit between 1 and 6 you mentally multiply this by 7 to determine which digit will be the unit digit in his product. You then pick up the slate and erase (if necessary) with your right thumb all digits up to this unit digit. With your left thumb you erase (if necessary) whatever remaining excess numbers which must be eliminated. Only four numbers must be erased, to leave you with the proper cycloid which will equal your spectator's product.

(6) the numbers game

This is a simple game played with numbers. It has a most intriguing feature: *you* can't lose!

The rules are as follows:

(a) Only two players at a time.

(b) Player "A" mentions any number that is not greater than 10. Player "B" mentions any number that is not greater than 10, and this is added to "A's" number. This process continues until 100 is reached, each player adding to the growing total.

(c) Whoever is the first to reach 100 is the winner.

(d) Following the sure-fire system discussed below will *always* make you the winner!

The system is based upon "key" numbers. You will not have to memorize these "keys" as they fit into a pattern which will be obvious to you. The "keys" are as follows: 12, 23, 34, 45, 56, 67, 78, and 89. You will note that to the first number, 12, you add 11 to bring it to the second "key." To the second "key" and to each succeeding "key" the number 11 is added.

Have your opponent select a number not greater than 10. To this number you appear to add a random number. Actually, the number you mention should bring the total to the first "key" when added to your opponent's number. As an example, let us assume that your opponent selects 7 as his first choice. You name 5, bringing the total to 12 (first "key").

Your opponent now adds another number to the total 12. Let us assume that he names 4, making the total 16. You must now bring the total to your second "key" 23. Thus, to 16 you must add 7, so you call 7 as your selection. This is continued until you arrive at your last "key," 89. Of course, at this point it is impossible for your opponent to reach 100 (since the maximum he can add to 89 is 10). After he mentions his number *you* can bring the total to 100—an ideal position.

The above theory can also be applied to dice, and other items. With dice usually one die is used, and the object is to reach a predetermined total . . . for example, 33. The first to reach 33 would win. A player turns the die so that the number he chooses shows on the top surface. Then the second player turns the die so that the number he wishes to use appears on the top surface. This is continued until 33 (or whatever predetermined total is agreed upon) is reached. Using a die limits to 6 the maximum number either may add to the total at one time. (Of course, this is because 6 is the highest number to appear on a die.)

To determine the "keys" you simply subtract 7 from 33 (assuming that 33 is the predetermined total). 7 from 33 leaves 26, thus 26 is the last "key." Subtracting 7 from 26 gives us 19, and 19 is the next to last "key." The next "key" is 12 (7 subtracted from 19), and the first "key" is thus 5. The "keys" are found in descending order. Since the highest number on a die is 6 then this number plus 1 results in 7, which is the amount by which your "keys" must progress to give you control of the game. (Note: In the 100 game system the "keys" advanced by 11—10 plus 1, the 10 being the maximum progression each player could make per turn.) Using this system will permit you to adopt the principle to any predetermined total, and any progressive value that you wish. Try it . . . you can't help but win!

Chapter 2

the magic of shape

One of the more esoteric fields of geometry is topology. Topology is concerned with the properties of figures that remain unaltered regardless of how the figure is contorted, twisted, stretched or compressed. Of course, the figure must not have any part broken off from it or new parts added.

For example, visualize a rubber doughnut that can be pulled, stretched and deformed in any way you please until it is out of shape. The doughnut will still retain its hole. Thus, although the shape of the doughnut has been changed the *property* of having one hole in the figure has not changed. The hole is a topological property.

Approximately 100 years ago a German mathematician by the name of Ferdinand Moebius was one of the first to become interested in topological properties of structures. He discovered a one-sided one-edged surface. The following pages will discuss this and many other topological forms that have entertaining applications in Mathematical Magic.

(1) The moebius strip

The Moebius Strip is a structure having one side and one edge. It is difficult to imagine a form of this sort, but in a few moments you will not only fully understand the Moebius Strip, but you will also be able to reproduce one.

If you were to take a strip of paper 1″ wide and 12″ long and glue the ends of the paper together you would form a ring or continuous loop, as pictured here:

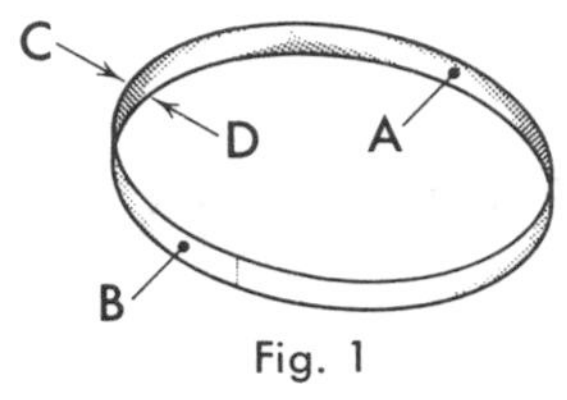

Fig. 1

This ring has two surfaces—an inner surface and an outer surface—and two edges. If you were to touch the inner surface, "A," and wanted to reach the outer surface without lifting your fingers from the ring, you would have to pass over either edge "C" or edge "D." (Edges "C" and "D" are limited in thickness, of course, but they are still two distinct and separate surfaces.)

Using the same strip of paper, 1″ wide and 12″ in length, by giving one of the edges a half twist before gluing the edges together, the result (after gluing the edges together) would be like the Moebius Strip shown below:

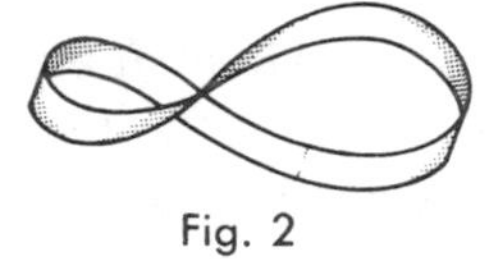
Fig. 2

This is a one-sided and one-edged structure. What is the proof of this statement? We know that with a conventional ring, as in fig. 1, it is necessary to cross an edge (either "C" or "D") to reach from one side to the other. However, with a Moebius Strip there is but one side: simply take a pencil and begin drawing a line along the side. You will find that you will draw a continuous line that completely covers the entire surface of the strip without ever having to cross an edge to reach the other side. Thus, the Moebius has one side. The conventional ring, in fig. 1, has two edges ("C" and "D"). To pass from one edge to the other you would have to cross either side "A" or side "B." But the Moebius has but one edge. Again, to prove this, draw a line along the edge of the Moebius Strip until you return to your starting point. As in the case of the side surface of the Moebius, you will have drawn a continuous line that completely covers the entire edge of the strip. Thus, the Moebius has but one side and one edge!

If you were to take the ring, as in fig. 1, and cut or tear it into halves along the center of the 1″ wide surface, you would end with two separate rings, each being ½″ wide and 12″ in length, as follows:

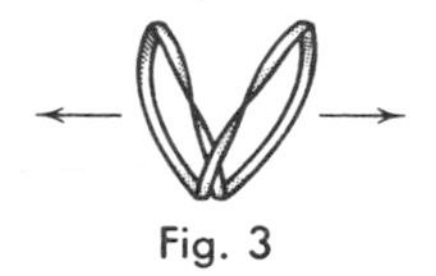

Fig. 3

The Moebius, being a one-sided surface, can't be cut or torn in half to form two separate rings. What would be the result of cutting or tearing the Moebius Strip along its center? The net result would be a large ring, ½″ in width and 24″ in length, shown here:

Fig. 4

(Note that there are half twists retained in the large ring.)

What are the properties of a strip having a full twist? A strip with a full twist is not a Moebius Strip, but it does have interesting possibilities. The strip with a full twist, though eccentric, has two edges and one inner and one outer surface. Let us assume that we put a full twist in a strip and then glued the edges together. Upon cutting or tearing this structure along the center of its width the result would be the two following inter-locked rings:

Fig. 5

Each ring would be ½″ wide and 12″ in length. (Note that each of the inter-locked rings has full twists within themselves.)

You may carry this further and experiment with additional twists and/or half twists, but these figures become more complex as the number of twists increase. For example, forming a strip with a twist-and-a-half will make the strip an eccentric Moebius (one-side and one-edge). Two full twists and the strip reverts to a more conventional structure of having two sides and two edges. But, as mentioned above, cutting or separating these strips results in tangled and knotted strips of little interest.

James C. Wobensmith is credited with applying the principles of these various combinations to a magical effect (*Greater Magic,* page 860, 3rd edition).

To show this informally, you can make simple paper strips and glue them together with rubber cement or a quick drying adhesive. To show this before a large group it is suggested that a linen fabric such as cambric be used instead of a strip of paper. A bright red or blue is colorful, and will suit the purpose.

To perform this you display what would appear to be a band of red linen material, about 2½″ wide and 30″ in length (the color, width, length, and type of material uscd can be varied to suit your needs.) An interesting approach would be to discuss the problems a circus property man has with seeing that all of the performers are always properly garbed. You could say the following:

"I met a fellow who worked for a circus, and his job was to be sure that all of the various acts were always clothed correctly. One of his most hectic experiences happened before the opening show of the tour the circus made last year. All of the performers were supposed to be dressed in the same costumes for the opening parade around the circus rings. At the last moment, just before the big parade, the circus barker rushed up to the property man and said, 'We need additional belts. Two of the acts have lost the belts used on their costumes.' The belts were bright red and similar to this material," you say as you show the band of red linen.

"My friend had just one band of belt material left. So he simply tore it in half, into two belts, just like this." As these words are said, you tear the band of material into two separate rings, appearing as in fig. 3.

You continue by saying: "The barker said, 'No, no! You don't understand. One of the acts is the fat lady.' Well, my friend said that would make it difficult, but that he'd do his best. And he did!" As you say this your spectators see you tear one of the rings into a very large ring, similar in appearance to fig. 4, thus solving the problem of the belt for the fat lady.

"This should have satisfied the barker, but he said, 'Now we've got a real tough one to solve, because the other act is the Siamese Twins!' Completely undaunted my friend rose to meet this emergency by doing this . . ." As these last words are said, the remaining ring is torn to result in two interlocked rings, as in fig. 5, which nicely concludes this effect.

The above comments are an ideal adaptation of remarks to the action. This can be a very amusing sequence of events.

To prepare for a demonstration as outlined above let us assume that you are using a fabric that is 2½″ wide and 30″ long. The ends of the material must be prepared before by sewing or gluing them together into a ring.

Place the ends before you, as shown here:

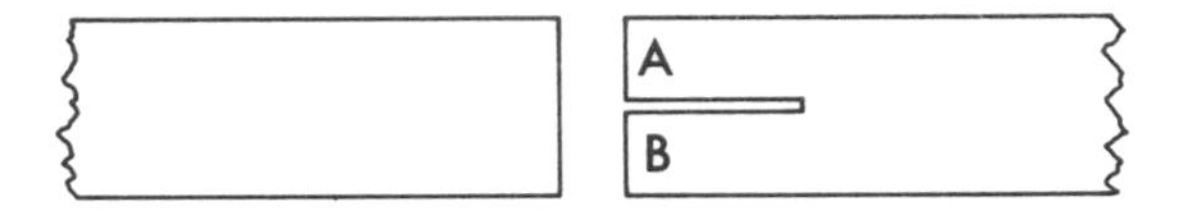

With a sharp pair of scissors cut a sliver out of the material at the right end that is about ⅛″ wide and about 2″ deep. You will note that the right end now has what we may refer to as two tabs, and we will call the upper tab "A" and the lower tab "B." Give tab "A" a half-twist and sew or glue it to the upper surface of the left end of the piece of cloth:

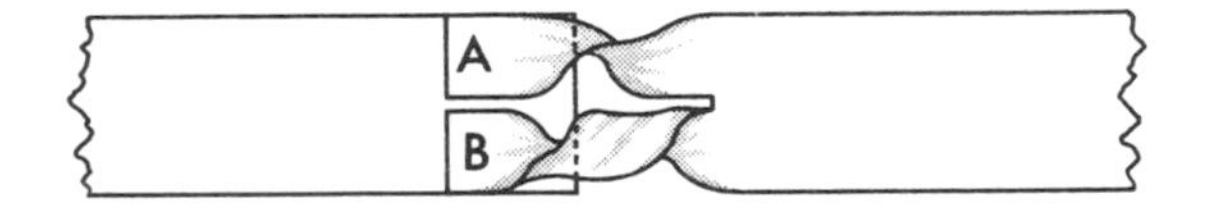

Give tab "B" a full twist and glue or sew it to the lower surface of the end.

This next preparation is made to assist you when you tear the rings apart. Without these little aids, it is quite difficult to start a tear in material. This is similar to the difficulty of starting a tear in the center of a piece of cellophane. Once a small start is made it is extremely simple to tear cellophane, but without the start it is quite difficult. Your first step is to remove a ⅛″ wide sliver from the center of the left end of the material. (This will assist you in your initial tear of the one ring into two separate rings.)

The next step is to cut a slit about 1″ long into the center of tab "A" and another slit 1″ long into the center of tab "B." (These last two cuts will assist you in cleanly concluding the last two tears in this effect.) The prepared end of the cloth, after all of the above preparation, will appear as follows:

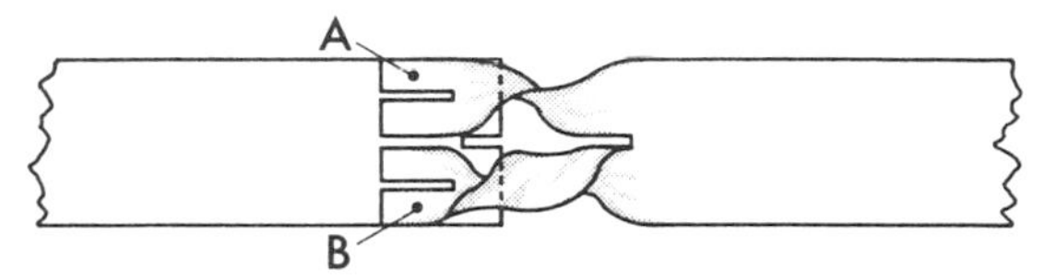

In performing, your right hand should be over the prepared part of the loop of cloth so that your spectators will suspect no preparation. As each tear is made, each hand should mask or cover the prepared sections of the loop as you perform the actions. Do not go directly into each tear but, gripping a piece of the loop in each hand (each hand masking the preparation), make the tear appear to take some effort.

After the first tear, into two separate loops, place the loop that has tab "B" over one of your arms so that you may first deal with the tab "A" loop. After successfully making the belt for the fat lady you may toss this to one of your spectators as a keep-sake. Then conclude your demonstration with the inter-locked rings. This, too, may be given away at the conclusion of your demonstration.

An interesting result, using a half-twist Moebius Strip, was suggested to me by Martin Gardner. If you have a Moebius Strip, and start to cut it by starting ⅓ in from an edge, and continue cutting ⅓ from the edge until it separates, the result will be two linked rings with one of the rings being twice the diameter of the smaller ring. (The smaller ring, of course, will be twice the width of the larger ring.) From this position you may continue and cut rings within rings, if you wish. For example, if you were to cut the smaller ring into equal halves the result would be two linked rings of equal diameter and width. If instead of cutting the smaller ring in half you cut it ⅓ from its edge, the result would be two large rings interlinked plus one small ring linked around the two large rings! You may discover unusual combinations by carrying this further.

(2) the tabor handkerchiefs

A mathematical-magician by the name of Edwin Tabor created a most interesting penetration effect using two solid objects—two handkerchiefs—which is purely topological in nature. It creates a wonderful illusion of the handkerchiefs literally melting through one another and it will appeal to the performer as well as to the spectators.

To learn to do this correctly you should follow each step with handkerchiefs in your hands. Men's pocket handkerchiefs are the best size.

(a) Pick up one of the handkerchiefs by holding a diagonally opposite corner in each hand, and twirl the handkerchief to form it into a tight rope-like shape. Do this with the second handkerchief so that each will appear as follows:

(b) Place one handkerchief over your left finger-tips in an east-west direction. Place the other on top of it, but in a north-south direction. The handkerchiefs should appear as shown below:

With your left thumb gently holding the handkerchiefs at the point where they cross each other.

(c) Your right hand grasps the north end of the upper handkerchief and wraps it once around the east-west handkerchief:

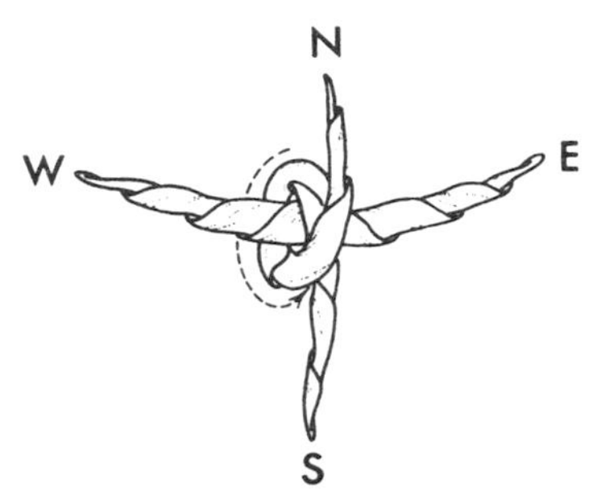

(d) With your right hand grasp the west end of the east-west handkerchief and wrap it once around the north-south handkerchief:

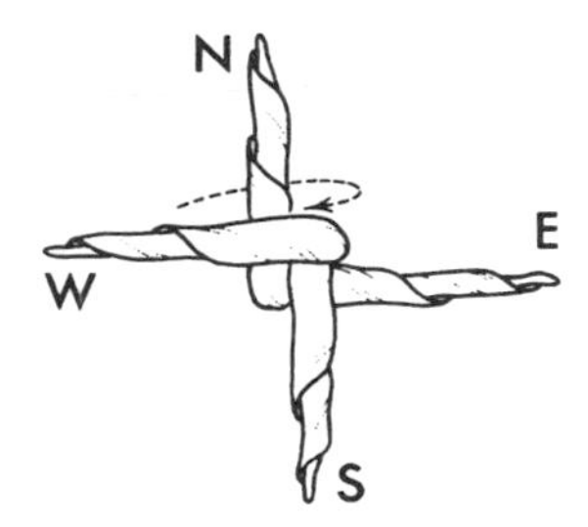

(e) Grasp the east and the west ends of the east-west handkerchief with your right hand, and the north and south ends of the north-south handkerchief with your left hand:

(f) Slowly pull your hands apart and the handkerchiefs will appear to melt through each other.

As mentioned above, it is essential that each step be carefully followed to successfully perform this stunt. What actually occurs is that the first curve (wrap) actually confines the two surfaces, tying one around the other.

The second wrap appears to add an additional band but actually places the second curve adjacent to the first curve (wrap). To understand the operation in its barest form I suggest that you follow the steps as given above, but substitute a piece of soft rope in place of one of the handkerchiefs. By doing this you will clearly see the action of the release. Of course, when demonstrating this before your friends you must use two handkerchiefs to achieve the proper illusion. The bulk of the handkerchiefs nicely conceals the true action.

(3) the jumping rubber band

An old stunt, the jumping rubber band, is well worth showing now that a new twist (no topological pun intended) has been added. To your on-lookers it would appear that you have a rubber band at the base of the third and fourth fingers of your right hand (fig. 6). Your fingers are closed into a loose fist, (fig. 7), and upon opening your fingers the rubber band jumps from its position in fig. 6, to your first and second fingers (fig. 8).

The new twist on this stunt is the addition of literally locking-in the rubber band. Two rubber bands are required. The first rubber band is placed over the third and fourth fingers of your right hand, as in fig. 6, and the second rubber band is twisted about each of your extended right finger-tips (fig. 9). Thus, you are locking-in the first band—it can't be removed from its position at the base of your third and fourth fingers. However, with the locking band, you once again make a loose fist, extend your right fingers, and lo!—the band again

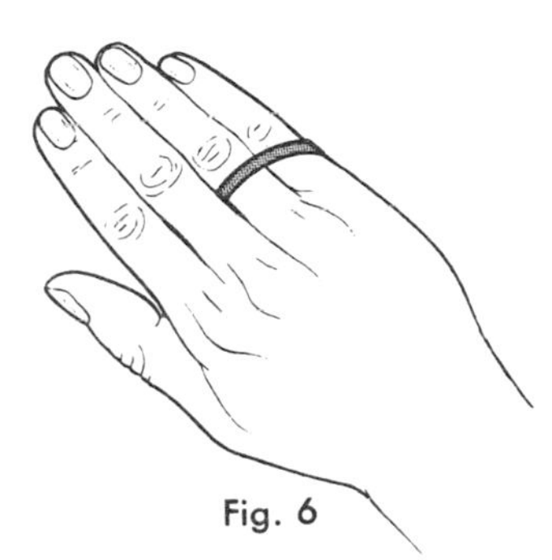

Fig. 6

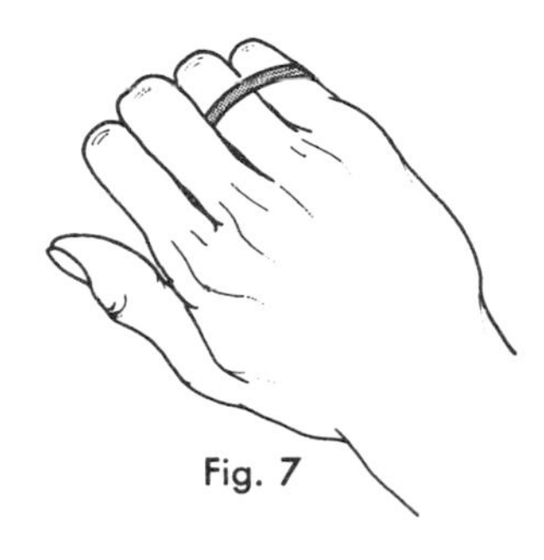

Fig. 7

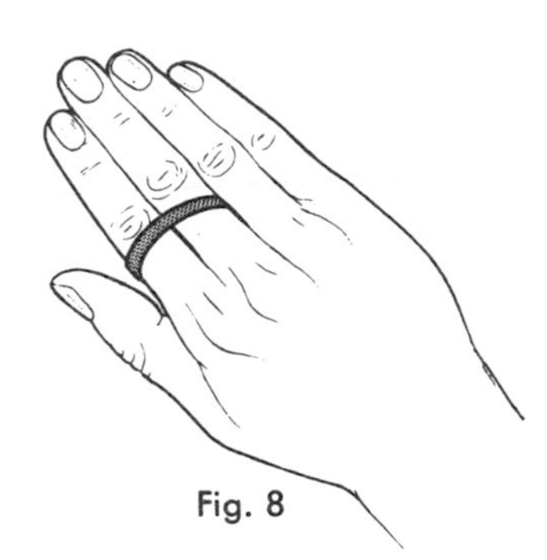

Fig. 8

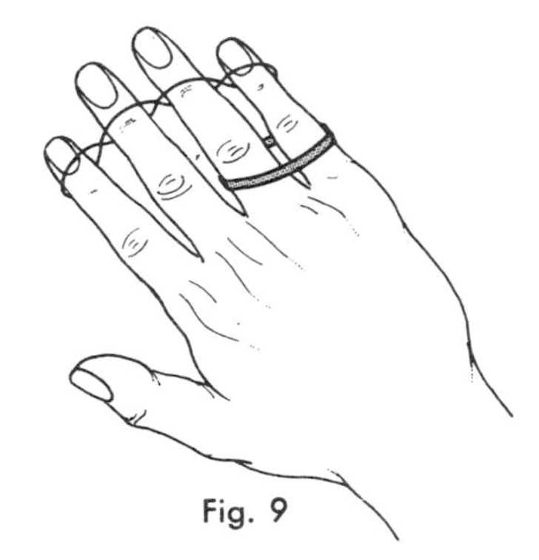

Fig. 9

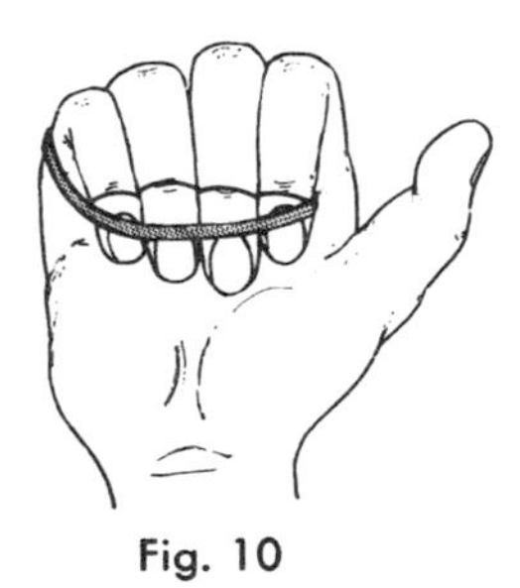

Fig. 10

successfully jumps from its position in fig. 9, to your first and second fingers.

Take a rubber band and closely follow the method for performing the first phase of this impromptu stunt:

(a) Place the band in position as in fig. 6.

(b) Extend your right fingers, with your right palm towards the floor.

(c) With your left fingers, lift the rubber band and pull on it to show that it is around your third and fourth fingers. Gently replace the rubber band and turn your right hand palm upwards.

(d) Your left fingers again lifts the band up (but this time your right hand is palm upwards) to show the band is still secured around your right third and fourth fingers.

(e) Follow this closely: Your left fingers are still stretching the rubber band a few inches off your right palm. Start to turn your right hand palm downwards, and as you turn your right hand over close your right fingers into a loose fist. Your left fingers (which are holding the extended band) turn to a position placing it under your right fist and gently releases the rubber band and drops away from your right fist. If this has been done correctly you will have loaded the rubber band across the tips of your right fingers. Your spectators should not be aware of this and it should have appeared to them that you have simply turned your right hand over and into a fist. Your right hand should appear as in fig. 7, but the true condition of the rubber band is indicated in fig. 10, an exposed view. This step should be done smoothly.

(f) Snap your left fingers and at the same time extend your right fingers. The rubber band will appear to magically jump from its position in fig. 6 to that in fig. 8.

To perform the second phase, place the first rubber band at the base of your right third and fourth fingers, as in fig. 6, then lock it in with the second rubber band by placing the second rubber band around your finger-tips as in fig. 9. Note that the band is given a twist as it is placed around each of your four finger-tips.

By following the exact same sequence of moves as outlined in steps "a" through "f" you will be able to duplicate the jumping effect even though you appear to have the extra hindrance of the locking band. Actually, the locking band at your right finger-tips does not in any way change the action or the result! It is just "window dressing."

A few trials with this stunt will soon reveal to you that the band doesn't actually jump from one position to the other. It simply revolves about a fulcrum, the pivot-point being the position at the base of and between your right second and third fingers.

Note that you can make the band jump from your first and second fingers back to its original starting position. But I suggest that you perform the effect using the simple sequence as suggested above: first make the single band jump from one position to the other and then "lock in" the single band and still successfully make it jump.

An interesting little story can be told, when showing this stunt, to add to its effectiveness. Discuss how a friend of yours lives in West Berlin and how he used to visit East Berlin by simply jumping over whenever he wished. Have the rubber band represent your friend, your right third and fourth fingers West Berlin, and your first and second fingers East Berlin. Place the rubber band (your friend) in West Berlin (over your right third and fourth fingers), perform the necessary steps to make "him" jump over to East Berlin. After this first phase, mention how the Russians had the "wall" put up to discourage free travel and entry into East Berlin. Perform the second phase of the stunt by having the second rubber band represent the "wall." Show that your friend, being of unusual ability, could still make the jump despite this cumbersome obstacle. "My friend is now educating as many people in East Berlin as he can as to how he does it. You probably read about his converts every day," your concluding remarks could well be.

There are many applications of topological principles with rubber bands, but this use is one of the more direct and effective items.

(4) the linking clips

This is an interesting transference of a curve. The idea is credited to Bill Bowman, of Seattle, Washington, and requires nothing more than a dollar bill and two paper clips.

Borrow a dollar bill and two paper clips. An applicable story-line would be to represent the paper clips as a Romeo-Juliet pair: a boy and a girl who care for each other but who are kept apart by their families.

You say, "The families of the boy (showing one of the clips) and the girl (displaying the other clip) wanted to keep this young couple apart. They lived next to each other, their homes separated by a wall. The dollar bill will represent the wall separating them." One side of the bill is folded and one of the clips is placed in position as in fig. 11. "The girl was locked in her room, which this will represent," you say, as you openly show the condition as in fig. 11. "The boy was also locked in his room, which was on the other side of the wall." As you make this last comment you gently fold the other side of the bill and place the second clip in position, as indicated in fig. 12. The second clip will bring "x" and "y" together.

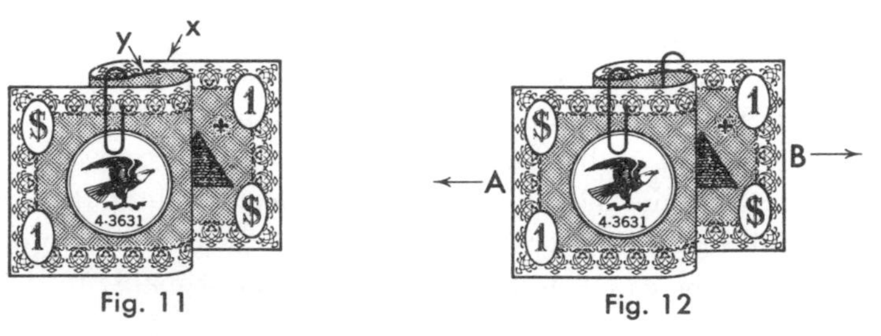

Fig. 11

Fig. 12

"Nothing is stronger than young love, and as you will soon see, the two could not be separated." As this is said you hold end "A" of the bill with your left hand, and "B" with your right hand. With a steady motion draw your hands apart until the bill is almost stretched out to its complete length. Then snap the bill smartly. The two clips will join one another, becoming linked, and they will literally pop off the bill.

If you closely follow the above instructions the entire action is self-working. What actually occurs is a transference of the curves in the bill to the clips so that the two clips link together. The originator of this idea, Mr. Bowman, uses a gold-plated and a silver-plated set of clips in performing this effect. These are carried in a leather pouch and these touches add tremendously to the dramatic effect of this miniature story.

(5) the shoe laces

Knots may be considered topological figures. G. W. Hunter, an English magician, developed the following idea into an amusing effect.

Basically, you form a typical bow-tie knot such as used when tying shoe laces. On pulling on the ends of the lace the knot will, of course, fall out. You again form the knot, but before pulling on the ends you place an end through each of the bows or loops. Normally, this will cause the knot to lock so that it can't slip out. But you successfully make the knot slip out smoothly just as you did without the additional "lock" knots.

I suggest that a length of soft white rope be used, about 24″ long. You must first form a double bow-knot. Do this as follows:

(a) With your right hand grasp one end of the rope about 8″ from its end. Your right hand should hold the rope with its palm towards the floor.

(b) Grasp the other end of the rope, about 8″ from the end, with your left hand. But your left hand should be held palm upwards, the rope resting on your upturned palm. Your position at this point should be as shown below:

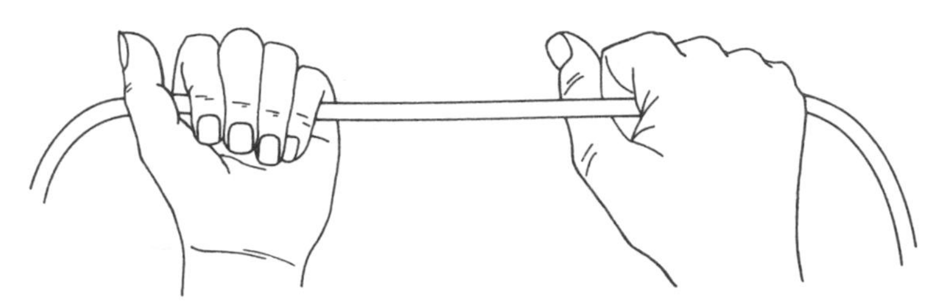

(c) Form your hands into loose fists, and twist your wrists so the finger-tips of each hand face each other. Thus, your left hand will turn a quarter turn to the right, and your right hand will also turn a quarter turn to the right. Your hands should appear as follows:

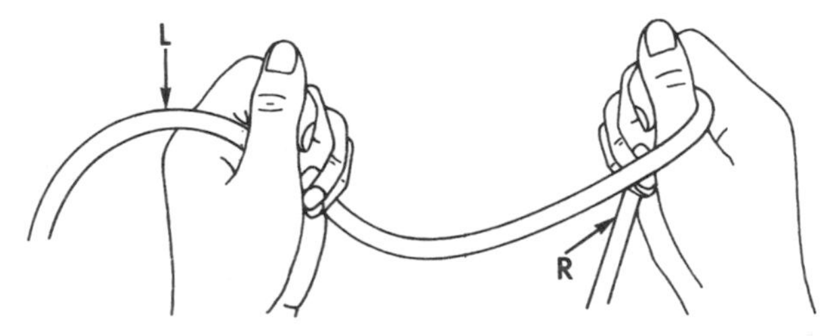

(d) Extend the first and second fingers of each hand. With the first and second fingers of your right hand grip section "L" of the rope.

(e) With the first and second fingers of your left hand grip section "R" of the rope.

(f) Begin to separate your two hands, but retain the ropes between the first and second fingers of each hand as you do so. (Release whatever other holds you may have on the rope.) Upon the separation of your hands you will have formed a double bow-knot, as shown below. Your left first and second fingers will be holding the bow-knot at point "A," and your right fingers will be holding it at point "B" in fig. 23.

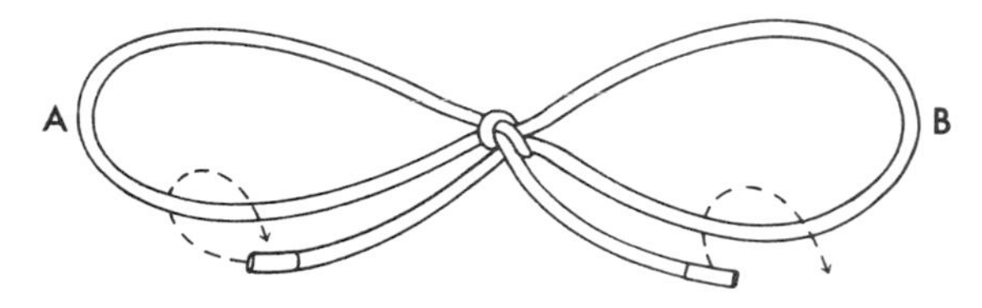

Steps "a" through "f" can be performed, after a few trials, in a matter of seconds. If you were to pull on the opposite ends of the rope the bow-knot would, of course, simply slip out. A suggested line of comment, as you form the double bow-knot, would be as follows: "My nephew is an active four-year-old, and one of the main problems in his life is that his shoe laces keep untying. (You should have completed the formation of the double bow-knot by this time.) This is what happens to him all day long." As you say this you simply pull the ends of the rope apart and the double bow-knot will dissolve, as anticipated.

"To solve the problem of tying his shoes all day I devised the following scheme." As this is said you again form a double bow-knot. "I simply slipped an end of the rope through each loop." As you say this you pass the left end of the rope through the left loop, and the right end of the rope through the right loop. Note that the ends are slipped from the back of the loops through to the front (towards you), as shown in the above figure. (When you form the double bow-knot, the right loop will tend to twist downwards. Be sure to avoid this twist, because the knot will lock if the end of the rope is passed through the right loop and you permit the loop to twist. Keep both loops flat and pass the ends through each flat loop.)

"Now the laces would not untie during the day. The big problem came at night as, being only four, the little boy would have trouble untying the knot. But I solved this by telling him that, when he wanted to remove his shoes at night, all he had to do was say the magic word:

TOPOLOGY, and he would have no trouble." As this is said simply pull the ends of the rope apart and the rope will form a knot bunched together in the center of the rope. At this point give the rope a sharp snap and the knot will dissolve, just as did the simple bow-knot.

Again, the effect is self-working and will require nothing more than your closely carrying out the steps as outlined above. The insertion of the ends of the rope through the loops will not result in a locked knot as the formation of the knot makes each loop an open curve. However, if *only* one end is placed through one loop and the rope is pulled taut a knot will form since one end will tend to close a curve. Thus, both ends must be passed through each of their respective loops. One additional thought is that you may pass the ends through the loops several times instead of just once. This may add to the effectiveness of the demonstration and will not interfere in the successful conclusion. But as mentioned above, it is essential that each end be passed through its loop the exact number of times as the other. If you fail to do this the rope will knot.

(6) houdini's coat escape

One of the greatest showmen to appear on the international stage was Harry Houdini. Today, more than 36 years after his passing he is still remembered and extolled for his sensational escape stunts. Basically, Houdini was a magician and his thinking and methods were that of a magician. The topological principle upon which this stunt is based was known and used by Houdini (and other performers) in various ways.

Using a man's jacket, two pieces of rope, and a coat hanger you perform an escape that is entirely impromptu and quite effective.

You may borrow the above items. The ropes should be about 9 feet in length. You can use the following remarks as you perform the various actions:

"Let us have this jacket (the borrowed jacket) represent Houdini, and these ropes will be used to securely bind him so that he can't effect an escape." Place the ropes over the hanger, (fig. 13), and continue: "I'll secure the ropes to the hanger." Tie the ropes together, in a simple knot, (fig. 14).

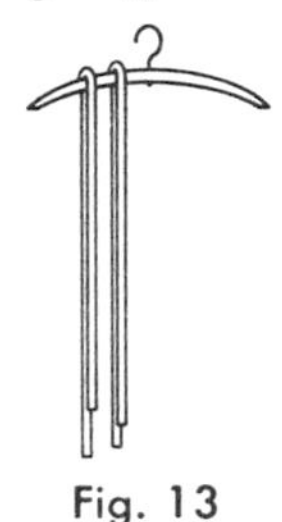

Fig. 13

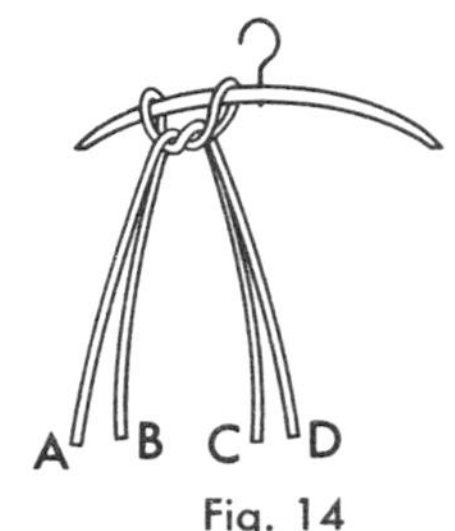

Fig. 14

At this point have the jacket placed on the hanger in the conventional manner you would use in hanging the jacket up for storage. "I would like you to be certain that Houdini, the jacket, is properly secured. Therefore, would you please place the ropes through each sleeve." Have your spectators place a pair of ropes through each sleeve. Ends A and B will thus be placed through the right jacket sleeve, and ends C and D through the left jacket sleeve (fig. 15).

"Let us now go a step further," you say, "Let us tie an additional knot to be sure the great man can't escape." Pick up one of the ends which is dangling from the right sleeve, and one of the ends from the left sleeve. Tie these together in a simple knot (fig. 16). To all appearances "Houdini" will be securely bound.

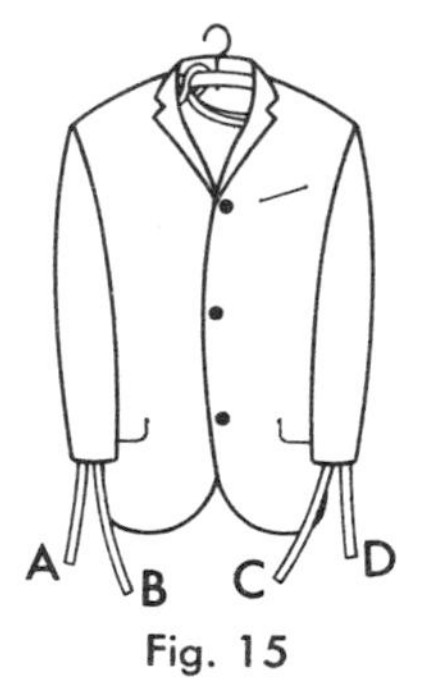

Fig. 15

Fig. 16

Request that a spectator hold two of the ends to your left, and another spectator hold the other two ends to your right. Remove the hanger by simply sliding it free from the ropes: grasp the rope at the point where the "knot" is formed with one hand, as your other hand slides the hanger free. The jacket will be supported by the hand which holds the "knot" (which has just been slid from the hanger) and by the ropes coming out of each sleeve (which are being supported by your two assistants).

"When I count three I want you to both pull on the ends of the ropes you are holding. Ready? One, two, three!" As this is said your spectators will pull on their ends. Release your grip on the "knot" and the jacket will become free, thus completing its escape. (Note, you should hold the jacket by the collar with your free hand to keep it from falling to the floor.)

The formation, as outlined above, actually results in two adjacent loops of rope being held together by the first knot you installed (fig. 14). Upon removing the hanger, the two loops will fall free. The ends of the rope coming out of each sleeve, as in fig. 15, are actually ends of the same piece of rope. The simple knot put in, in fig. 16, is necessary so that after the escape has been made each spectator winds up holding two ends of opposite ropes. If this extra knot wasn't put in, each spectator would wind up with the ends of the same rope in his hands . . . a loop. Thus, this extra knot is a device for crossing-over the ropes.

A very fine performer by the name of Dante performed a stunt using this same principle in his full evening show. In place of a coat hanger he used a cane upon which he tied the two cords. In place of a jacket he tied colorful handkerchiefs and bangles on each side of the ropes. After putting in the extra knot, as in fig. 16, he would withdraw the cane from the ropes and the handkerchiefs and bangles would escape from the ropes in a colorful manner.

Note: If you were to tie white handkerchiefs on each side of the cane *before* putting in the extra knot, and if you were to tie blue handkerchiefs onto the ropes *after* putting in the extra knot, upon removing the cane the white handkerchiefs would fall free and thus "escape" while the blue ones would still be tied to the ropes. This opens up many unusual presentations should you wish to develop this theme in greater depth.

(7) rope monte

The clever mathematician-magician, Dr. L. Vosburgh Lyons,* developed the handling about to be described in this "con game." Basically, it is a betting proposition that appears to offer the sucker a 50–50 chance of winning. Actually, it is under the complete control of the operator. For entertainment purposes it can provide much amusement as your spectators try to outwit you . . . they don't know that it is impossible for you to lose!

An offshoot of the "Figure 8" game, this requires nothing more than a piece of rope, an understanding of the principle, and a few moments of serious practice so that you can perform it smoothly.

A piece of soft white rope, four or five feet in length, is suitable. Hold the two ends in your left hand, and the center loop in your right hand. Place the rope on the table and with your right hand form the shape as indicated in fig. 17. For clarity each single strand of rope has been given a number, 1 through 6. The center of the rope, Y, is pushed to position X.

Pick up strand 4 with your left fingers, and pick up strand 5 with your right fingers. Exchange positions so that strand 4 is now alongside of strand 6 (which has not been moved), and strand 5 is alongside of strand 3 (which is also undisturbed) (fig. 18). Note that this roughly

* This was first published in Bruce Elliott's magical periodical, "The Phoenix."

resembles an 8. It has two circles, an upper and a lower circle. You may clarify this by making each circle more distinct and the entire figure closer to the appearance of an 8.

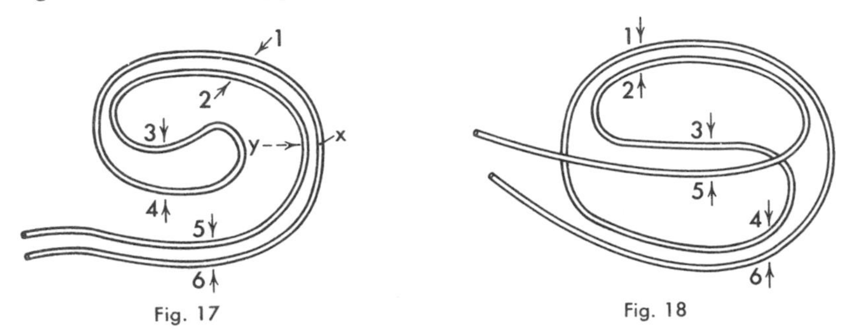

Fig. 17

Fig. 18

The object is for your spectator (or a bettor) to select one of the circles, the upper or the lower, and place his index finger into the center of the circle of his choice. You now grasp the ends of the rope and draw it away from the table. If he has selected the correct circle the rope will catch about his index finger—in which case he would "win." However, if the rope does not engage his finger but pulls freely off the table, then your spectator "loses."

If the rope is placed as in fig. 18, the upper circle will always fall free and the lower circle will always catch or engage the spectator's finger. (A few trials will make this apparent to you.) In demonstrating, your spectators will soon become aware of this.

It is at this point that you throw in the "convincer." You start to form the 8, as in fig. 18, but actually put a slight twist in the center loop as you place it down (fig. 19). (Strand 4 will now be in the position normally occupied by strand 3.) Strand 3 is placed alongside of strand 6, while strand 5 is placed alongside of strand 4 (fig. 20). Figures 18 and 20 will appear to be identical to the most discerning observer. But the slight variation makes the difference because with this put down neither the upper nor the lower circles can be winners! Regardless of which circle is chosen the rope will *always* draw free!

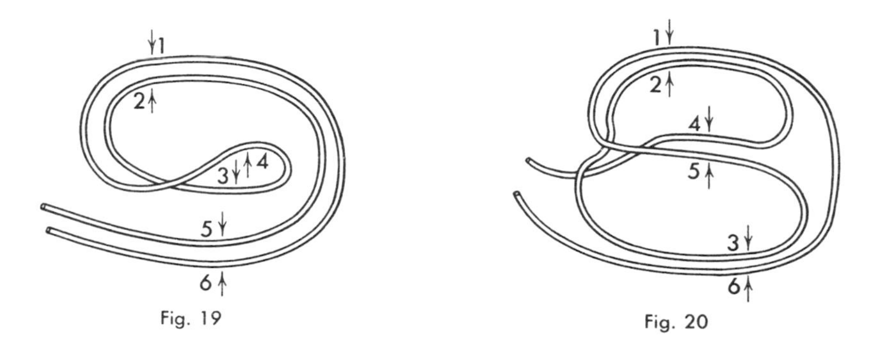

Fig. 19

Fig. 20

The slight "twist" in the rope results in two open circles (curves) so that neither will engage the spectator's finger. It is almost impossible to tell the fair and the false 8's apart.

It is essential that you spend the minimum of time necessary to learn to correctly place the rope down whether you are putting down the fair or the false 8. The action of each should be duplicates so that your spectators will see no variation or "hitch" during your demonstration.

This can be exceedingly puzzling to your on-lookers, and it is suggested that you don't constantly put down the false circles, as in fig. 20. Vary it so that occasionally your spectators do win, or so that you can prove that it is possible for them to win by putting your own finger in the lower circle when the fair 8 has been put down. As a matter of odds, if you alternate fair put downs with false, you will have a 3-1 continuous advantage . . . which isn't bad!

Present this as a simple betting game that has been used by carnival operators and small time grifters for years. You won't be departing too far from the truth!

Chapter 3

calendar magic

Our manner of living is assisted by many precise and mathematically perfect instruments. For example, our seconds, minutes, and hours are symmetrically perfect. Our weeks are also arranged in an orderly seven day pattern. Our months, however, are a more haphazard lot. We have one 28 day month . . . yet we advance this to 29 days every four years (leap year). We have four 30 day months and the balance are, of course, of 31 days duration. Even with this apparent lack of order there are many relationships which exist in our calendars, and which are exceedingly novel.

Some of these relationships may be quite obvious to you, but not to the average person. It is possible to become involved in complex mathematical structures with a calendar, but the material in this chapter has been confined to the lighter, less tenuous approach.

Many people, and several organizations of international importance, are dedicated to the adoption of a uniform and simplified calendar. Months of a uniform number of days is the main goal, with each month starting on the same weekday as each preceding month. And other orderly arrangements are also desired. Imagine the possibilities, mathematically speaking, with a calendar of this sort! However, using our present calendars (which are comparatively crude), I am sure you will find many interesting applications discussed in the following pages.

Several items will be discussed with more than one method given in explanation. I suggest that you learn only one at a time as it is possible for you to confuse one with another. If you become bored with the methods you are using you can always refer to this chapter and substitute other methods for those you no longer find interesting.

It is difficult to determine the originators of the various approaches to the "problems" which will be discussed. No doubt some of the world's earliest mathematicians noted the relationships inherent in the calendar. It will be possible for you to develop techniques, just as I have, independently; but others may well have covered the same ground.

To start, I would like to discuss the horizontal listings of the calendar. Any month and year, of course, may be used. Current calendars are used, at this writing, for convenience.

(1) horizontal figuring

A. Three Dates. It is possible for you to have any three consecutive dates selected, have these added together, and upon being given the total you immediately name the three chosen dates. Of course, it will appear obvious that with a hit-or-miss or trial-and-error approach you can work towards finding the correct combination of dates. But by using this simple system you can *immediately* determine the chosen dates.

Let us assume that your spectator has a calendar, and that he draws a circle around three dates.

1963			MARCH			1963
SUN	MON	TUE	WED	THU	FRI	SAT
					1	2
3	4	5	6	7	8	9
10	11	12	13	(14	15	16)
17	18	19	20	21	22	23
24	25	26	27	28	29	30
31						

In this case the 14th, 15th, and 16th would have been selected. Your spectator adds these three values together and tells you that the sum of the dates he chose is 45.

You simply divide the total by 3 (45 divided by 3 equals 15), and your result will always be the center date. Knowing that the center date is 15 you have but to subtract 1 to find the first date, and add 1 to it to find the last date.

For maximum effect, announce the correct dates as quickly as you can compute them. (Try this with another series of three consecutive dates to observe the simplicity of it.)

In showing this stunt it is possible that you will come in contact with someone who either does not understand your instructions, or who will intentionally misinterpret your remarks in an attempt to confuse you. Instead of circling three consecutive dates in a line they will circle three dates in a row, as follows:

1963			MARCH			1963
SUN	MON	TUE	WED	THU	FRI	SAT
					1	2
3	4	(5)	6	7	8	9
10	11	(12)	13	14	15	16
17	18	(19)	20	21	22	23
24	25	26	27	28	29	30
31						

Note that a row of three dates has been circled, the 5th, 12th, and 19th. You can still arrive at a satisfactory conclusion. The total of these three is 36, and upon being told this total you again divide by 3 (36 divided by 3 equals 12). The result, in this case 12, once again gives you the center date. To find the first date you simply subtract 7 from the center date, and to find the third date you just add 7 to the center date. Thus, you can overcome what would appear to be a difficult situation.

B. Four, Five, and Six. You can immediately determine the dates in any consecutive group of four, five, or six numbers. The systems are as follows:

Four: Given the sum of a series of four consecutive dates you divide the total by 4, and ignore any remainder. The result will be the *second* date in the series. As an example, if you are given the total 94 (the sum of 22, 23, 24, and 25) you divide this total by 4, which results in 23 and a remainder of 2. Ignore the remainder; 23 indicates the second date in the series. Knowing the second date, it is elementary to determine the other dates.

Five: A similar system applies for a series of five consecutive dates, only in this case you divide by 5 and the result of the addition tells you the date in the *third* position. Example, you are given the total 40 (the sum of 6, 7, 8, 9, and 10). 5 divided into 40 results in 8, which is the third date in the series. Simply deduct 2 from 8 to determine the first date and proceed as above.

Six: With a series of six dates you divide by 6 (ignoring any remainder) and the result is the *third* date of the series. Example, let us assume that you are given the total 129 (the sum of the following series: 19, 20, 21, 22, 23, and 24). Upon dividing 129 by 6 your result is 21 (ignoring the 3 left over), and 21 is the *third* date in the series. Knowing this, you can easily determine the other dates.

C. Seven Dates. You can carry this further, but I will describe two systems for a series of seven dates to conclude this section. Let us assume that you are given the total 182 (this is the sum of the following seven consecutive dates: 23, 24, 25, 26, 27, 28, and 29). Dividing the total by 7 will give you the *fourth* date in the series. In this case, 182 divided by 7 results in 26. Knowing that 26 is the *fourth* date, you simply subtract 3 to know that the first day in the series was the 23rd.

A method first described by the late Dr. Jacob Daley, an outstanding physician and mathematician-magician, utilizes the following procedure: with a series of seven numbers you first subtract 21 from the given total, and then divide the balance by 7. The result will be the *first* date in the series. To show how this operates, let us assume that you were given the total 182, as above. Subtracting 21 from 182 would leave you with 161, and dividing 161 by 7 results in 23. And this result, 23, is the first date in the series.

You may experiment with variations and other combinations should you wish to enlarge upon this theme. There are limitless ways to approach this.

(2) vertical figuring

Under the item titled Three Dates I discussed a method of determining three vertical dates. There are other combinations with vertical numbers and we will first deal with four numbers in a row.

Assume that your spectator has encircled four dates in a vertical row, and he has given you the total.

1963			APRIL			1963
SUN	MON	TUE	WED	THU	FRI	SAT
	1	2	3	4	5	(6)
7	8	9	10	11	12	(13)
14	15	16	17	18	19	(20)
21	22	23	24	25	26	(27)
28	29	30				

In this case the total would be 66 (the sum of 6, 13, 20, and 27). To find the *first* date in the series, the procedure is to subtract 42 from the total and then divide the remainder by 4. In this case, 42 subtracted from 66 leaves a remainder of 24, and 24 divided by 4 results in 6. Thus, 6 is the first date of the series. To find the second date you add 7 to the first date (13), and continue to add 7 to each succeeding date to determine the entire series of four dates.

A second method, for four vertical dates, is to divide by 4 (*and add in any remainder*), and then subtract 12. Using 66, as above, dividing this by 4 gives you 16 and a remainder of 2. Adding in the remainder brings you to 18 (16 plus the 2 remainder). Upon subtracting the constant 12 results in 6, which is the first date in the series. You now add 7 to it to find the second date in the series, and continue adding 7 for each subsequent date.

Let us move on to the addition of 5 vertical figures. Assume that a group of five figures are selected, as in the calendar below:

1963			APRIL			1963
SUN	MON	TUE	WED	THU	FRI	SAT
	1	2	3	4	5	6
7	8	9	10	11	12	13
14	15	16	17	18	19	20
21	22	23	24	25	26	27
28	29	30				

The total 80 would be given to you (2, 9, 16, 23, and 30). To determine the selected dates you must subtract 70 and divide the balance by 5. In this case 70 subtracted from 80 leaves 10, and 5 divides into 10 twice. Thus, 2 is the first date in the series. You add 7 to it to find the second date, and proceed as above for the other dates.

A second method for a vertical row of five figures is as follows: divide the total by 5 and subtract 14 to determine the first date in the series. Applying this system to the above example, upon being given the total 80 you divide by 5 (80 divided by 5 results in 16) and subtract 14 from the result (14 subtracted from 16 leaves 2). Thus, 2 is the first date in the series.

(3) squares and blocks

A. Four Square. Any square of four dates is circled and the total of the dates are added together. Upon being given the total you can immediately name the four chosen dates. Let us assume that a square is selected as that pictured below:

1963			MAY			1963
SUN	MON	TUE	WED	THU	FRI	SAT
			1	2	3	4
5	6	7	8	9	10	11
12	13	14	15	16	17	18
19	20	21	22	23	24	25
26	27	28	29	30	31	

You are given the total, which in this case is 56 (10, 11, 17, and 18). To be able to name the four dates you must first discover the value of the lowest date. To do this you divide the number by 4 and then subtract 4 from the result. Using 56, we divide this by 4, which gives us 14. Upon subtracting 4 from 14 we arrive at 10, which is the lowest date in the square. The next highest date is found by simply adding 1 to the lowest date. To find the third highest date simply add 7 to the value of the *first* date (10 plus 7 equals 17), and add 1 to the third date for the last date in the square.

Another system for a square of four dates is to subtract 16 from the given total and divide the remainder by 4. Applying this to the above example, 16 from 56 leaves 40, and 40 divided by 10 results in 10—the first date in the square.

B. Block of Nine. You may carry the above idea further by having a block of nine dates selected.

1963			MAY			1963
SUN	MON	TUE	WED	THU	FRI	SAT
			1	2	3	4
5	6	7	8	9	10	11
12	13	14	15	16	17	18
19	20	21	22	23	24	25
26	27	28	29	30	31	

Using the example above, you do not require a total of all of the nine dates! Instead, you only need the *sum* of any two of the dates which are diagonally opposite each other. Thus, your spectator will add together either 12 and 28 or 14 and 26. (Note that either diagonal pair will add to the same total!) In this example, you will be given the total 40. To determine the center number in the block you merely divide the total by 2. Thus, 40 divided by 2 results in 20, and 20 is the central date in the block. (This is the date in the fifth position.) Of course, to find the fourth date you simply subtract 1 from this date, and you add 1 to find the sixth date. You now add or subtract 7 from the fourth, fifth, and sixth dates to find the other dates.

Another interesting stunt using a block of nine numbers is to be able to name immediately the total of all nine dates upon being given the lowest date in the series. Let us use the above example of nine dates. You would be told that 12 is the lowest date in the selected series of nine. Upon being told this you request that your spectator add all nine numbers together. Before he actually starts his addition you announce the total: 180!

The system for accomplishing this is as follows: add 8 to the value given to you, and multiply the new total by 9. The result will be the total of the nine dates. In this case you add 8 to 12 (total of 20), and multiply this new total, 20, by 9 (20 times 9 results in 180). As mentioned above, this simple series of two steps can be done quite rapidly, which will greatly add to its effectiveness.

(4) rectangles

There are just two more variations that I will cover, and these are six-figure rectangles. Let us first deal with the figure which is two wide and three deep. Using the calendar below, this would include the dates 2, 3, 9, 10, 16, and 17.

1963			JUNE			1963
SUN	MON	TUE	WED	THU	FRI	SAT
						1
2	3	4	5	6	7	8
9	10	11	12	13	14	15
16	17	18	19	20	21	22
23	24	25	26	27	28	29
30						

Assume that your spectators have freely chosen and encircled this rectangle. Request that these dates be added together and that you be given the total. To determine the lowest date in the series you must subtract 45 from the total, and divide the remainder by 6. In this case you would be given the total 57 and, upon subtracting 45 from 57, you would arrive at a remainder of 12. Dividing 12 by 6 brings you to 2, and this is the lowest date in the series. The second date is found by adding 1 to the first date, and the other dates are found by progressions of 7, already explained.

Dealing with a six-figure rectangle that is three wide and two deep, the system employed to find the lowest date is to subtract 27 and divide by 6.

1963			JUNE			1963
SUN	MON	TUE	WED	THU	FRI	SAT
						1
2	3	4	5	6	7	8
9	10	11	12	13	14	15
16	17	18	19	20	21	22
23	24	25	26	27	28	29
30						

If you apply this, using the example above, you would be given the total 99 (the sum of 12, 13, 14, 19, 20, and 21). Subtracting 27 from 99 would leave you a remainder of 72, and dividing 72 by 6 results in 12, which is the lowest date in the series. You find the second and third dates by progressions of 1, and the other dates by progressions of 7.

As mentioned earlier, you can develop an endless variety of systems and combinations. If your appetite has been excited, I can assure you of many pleasant moments and the delight of personal discovery.

(5) the birthday paradox

For a change of pace, I would like to describe what is known as "The Birthday Paradox." Let us assume that you walked into a room in which there was a group of at least 24 people. What do you think are the probabilities that at least two of these people have the same birthday? At first reflection it appears remote since there are 365 days (plus one extra on leap years) of possibilities among a reasonably small group. Yet, if you were to bet anyone on an even money basis (50–50) you would have a better chance of winning than losing!

Mathematically, if you were to make this bet 50 times you would win 27 times and lose 23 times. Thus, you would have better than a 50% advantage on each individual bet. And this is based on only 24 people being in the room. As the number of the group increases your favorable percentage has a remarkable increase.

George Gamow, in his book *One, Two, Three—Infinity* offers this approach to arriving at this conclusion: the chance of any two people having the same birthday is 364/365 (one chance in 365). The chance of a third person differing from the other two is 363/365. This is carried forward until the 24th person develops the fraction 342/365. The 23 fractions are multiplied together to reach the probability that all 24 have different birthdays. The reduced product is the fraction 23/50. Thus, at least one coincidence of birthdays among 24 people will *not* occur 23 times out of every 50 trials, but *will* occur 27 times out of every 50 trials.

With a group of 30 people you will have, roughly, a 70–30 advantage of the incidence of at least two people being born on the same day. With 40 people your advantage rockets to a 90–10 advantage. With a group of 60 people you are extremely close to certainty. (Note that 100% certainty is not attained unless there are 366 people present.) To show you how strong the odds become, with a group of 100 people you would have an odds advantage of occurrence of approximately 3,300,000 to 1!

An amusing way to show this paradox is to introduce it in a group of at least 24 people. Pass slips of paper to each, and request that they each put down their birthday . . . not including the year. If you wish, you may suggest that they fake their real birthdates, if they wish, and put down *any* day as their birthday. (An imagined birthday, a preferred birthday over their actual birthday, the birthday of a friend . . . or any variation they desire.) As long as they make a random choice, and without collaboration, the probability will *not* be affected by this departure!

After the slips are collected you state that at least two people in the group have written the exact date. And this is proved when you open each slip and compare the birthdays listed.

As an example of this paradox, let us investigate the record of births and deaths of Presidents of the United States. Investigating 33 births and 30 deaths discloses that Polk and Harding were both born on November 2nd. Jefferson, Adams, and Monroe each died on July 4th. Using any series of records, you will find that the probabilities, as mentioned above, stand up very well.

An approach to a further understanding of the incidence inherent in this paradox is to first check A's birthday against B's. Assuming that they do not coincide we then take C's and check him against A's and B's. Still no match, so we check D's against A's, B's, and C's. With these four possibilities we have had 6 opportunities for a coincidence. By the time we have 10 people involved we will have had 45 opportunities for a coincidence! And the curve continues upward, with increasing velocity, as each additional person is added.

(6) days and dates

Let us assume that you were told that the 24th was a Friday. How could you immediately state what day of the week the 1st day fell on, and what day was the last day of the month?

This interesting problem depends upon the fact that the 1st day of each month and the 15th day of each month always fall on the same day. Thus, upon learning that the 24th was a Friday you must make a simple backward computation to get to the 15th. In this case you subtract 7 from 24, which tells you that the 17th was also a Friday (in this particular month). You now simply go back two days to the 15th, and you thus know that the 15th was a Wednesday and thus the 1st day of the month had to be a Wednesday. (Note; in this example, you simply had to deduct 7 to bring you to the 15th. In other cases you may have to go forward by adding 7 and then making up the difference.)

To determine the last day of the month the following table may be used:

28-day month . . . subtract 1 day from 1st day of month
29-day month . . . ends on same day as 1st day of month
30-day month . . . add 1 day to 1st day of month
31-day month . . . add 2 days to 1st day of month

Assuming that the month in the above example was a 31 day month, you would add 2 days to the 1st day of the month (Wednesday) and state that the month ended on a Friday. A simple and amusing problem.

(7) date choice

This is an intriguing idea which is dependent upon the numerical balance within our calendar listings. Walter Gibson was one of the first to describe this, in *The Jinx,* a magic magazine no longer published.

You offer your spectators a calendar and state, "I am going to turn away from you as I don't want to influence your choice. How many lines are there on this particular calendar page? (You will be informed that there are five lines.) I want you to put a circle around any date that appeals to you in the first line. And I want you to continue to circle one date in each line. You may select any date in each line which you desire."

Let us assume that your spectator has circled the dates indicated below:

1963			JULY			1963
SUN	MON	TUE	WED	THU	FRI	SAT
	(1)	2	3	4	5	6
7	8	(9)	10	11	12	13
14	15	16	(17)	18	19	20
21	22	23	24	25	26	(27)
28	(29)	30	31			

You now ask, "Did you circle any Sundays?" To this you will receive a negative reply. "Any Mondays?" He will reply yes, and so you inquire as to how many Mondays. Upon learning that two Mondays were circled, you then proceed to ask about each of the other days. This is all the information you require.

You now request that your spectator add together the numerical value of the five dates he has freely chosen. In this case, the total of the circled dates will be 83. After the addition has been completed you request that your spectator simply concentrate on this total. Point out that they have freely circled five dates, that your back has been turned away from your spectator all during this experiment, and that it is virtually impossible for you to have any idea as to the total he is now thinking of. After a few moments, you dramatically state, "I have a firm impression of the number 83; am I correct?" You will not only be right, but your spectators will be astonished!

The method is quite ingenious. Unknown to your spectators you use a calendar month that has five Wednesdays listed. Also, you have added the total value of the five Wednesdays beforehand, and you have secretly retained this total in your mind. In this case, the total of the five Wednesdays in the calendar month used totals 85. (Note that this can be accomplished without restriction of a month having five Wednesdays, but confining this to a five Wednesday month greatly simplifies the operation.)

You are now prepared to display this experiment, and you do so by offering the calendar month used above to your spectators. Have him follow your instructions by circling one date in each line. Let us assume that your spectator has made his selections as shown above.

You must now secretly add or subtract certain values, on the basis of the days your spectator has chosen. The following "scale" is used, and you may simply memorize this (as it follows an easy to remember pattern), or you may copy it and keep it on a business card. It will be simple enough for you to refer to when doing this experiment as you will be turned away from your spectators.

Sunday	*Monday*	*Tuesday*	*Wednesday*	*Thursday*	*Friday*	*Saturday*
−3	−2	−1	0	+1	+2	+3

The scale runs 3–2–1 to 0 and back up 1–2–3, but the values to the left are subtracted, and the values to the right are added.

Now to the operation: you recall 85 as your key number. You now ask if any Sundays were circled. Upon receiving a negative reply, your key remains unchanged. You ask about Mondays. Upon learning that two Mondays were circled you must subtract 4 from your key (−2 twice). Your key is now 81. Upon learning that one Tuesday was circled you must subtract 1 from your key so that your key is now 80. (You may ignore Wednesdays, if you wish, as regardless of whether or not any Wednesdays are circled you do not add or subtract anything.) Upon learning that, in this case, no Thursdays or Fridays were circled your key remains at 80. Upon learning that one Saturday was circled you must add 3, so your final key is 83. This will be the total value of the various dates circled.

Conclude your demonstration as suggested above. Add a little drama and your presentation will prove very impressive.

A simple way to explain the mechanics of this would be to assume that your spectator circled five Mondays. Of course, in actual practice this is very remote, but it will expose the relationship of the numbers to you. Using the same calendar again, the five Mondays total to 75. Your key is still 85. Upon learning that five Mondays were circled you would have to subtract 2 five times, or subtract 10 from your key. Thus, 10 from 85 leaves you with 75 . . . which equals the five circled Mondays.

Monday is two days removed from Wednesday. Thus, each Monday requires a subtraction of 2 from the Wednesday total. Sunday is three days removed, thus each Sunday requires a subtraction of 3 from the Wednesday total. Friday is two days beyond Wednesday, thus for each Friday you would have to add 2 days to the Wednesday total. The relationship should be very clear to you. The scattered dates, which will occur in the usual random selection, are compensated for by the addition or subtraction with the scale. This can be a puzzling demonstration.

(8) stover's prediction

The amiable mathematician-puzzle master, Mel Stover, was one of the first to describe this interesting prediction idea using a calendar. Any calendar is used and your spectators draw an outline around any 4 by 4 square of dates. Let us assume that a choice has been made as in the calendar below:

1963 **JULY** 1963

SUN	MON	TUE	WED	THU	FRI	SAT
	1	2	3	4	5	6
7	8	9	10	11	12	13
14	15	16	17	18	19	20
21	22	23	24	25	26	27
28	29	30	31			

At this point you turn away from your spectators and direct the proceedings so that you "can't influence your spectators." Before going further, however, you hand a slip of paper to one of the spectators requesting that this not be opened until the conclusion of this experiment.

Any spectator is requested to freely circle one of the dates in the square. Let us assume that he circles 26. This selection, and the others, is unknown to you. You now request that he draw a line through all of the vertical dates that appear above or below the date circled, and also all of the horizontal dates which are either to the left or right of the circled date. The condition should now appear as below:

3	4	5	6
10	11	12	13
17	18	19	20
24	25	26	27

Another date is secretly circled. Let us assume that this is 11. Again, the vertical and horizontal dates are crossed out:

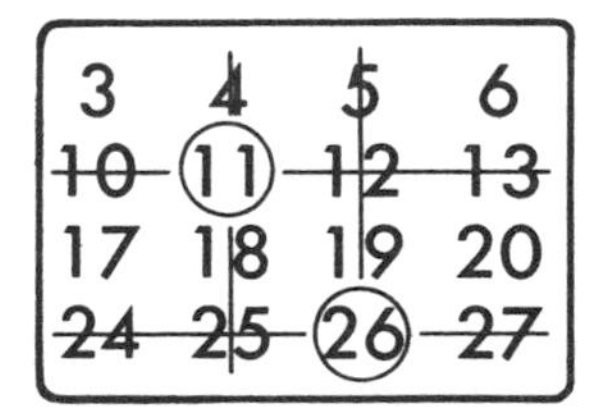

A third date is chosen, following the above procedure. When this has been done, only one date will remain which has not been circled or crossed out. Have the spectator circle this date. Assuming that the third date chosen was 6, the calendar will appear as follows:

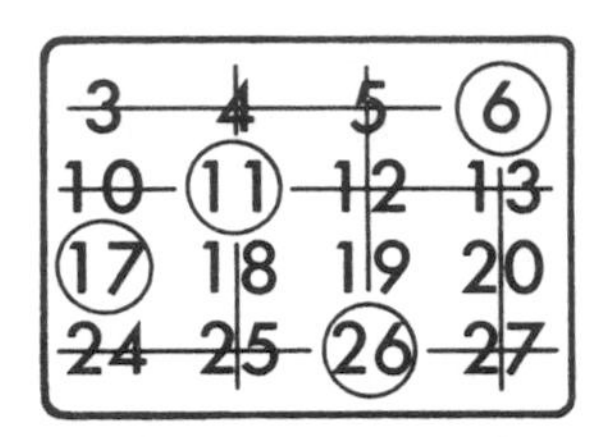

You now request that the four circled dates be added together. In this case, they will total to 60 (6, 11, 17, and 26). After your spectators have reached this total you turn towards them and say, "I wrote a prediction before the start of this experiment. The reason I turned away was that I did not want you to feel that I could in any way influence your selections. Now what is the total you have arrived at?" Upon learning that the total is 60 you have your prediction opened and on the slip of paper is written: "I predict that the total of the dates you choose will be 60!" An impressive climax.

By having your spectators eliminate vertical and horizontal listings, after the selection of each date, you are imposing a "force" of a related series of numbers! Your work is quite simple: as soon as the outline has been drawn around the square of 16 dates you simply look at any pair of diagonally opposite dates and add them together. In the above square, the total would be 30 (by adding together either 3 and 27, or 6 and 24). Upon learning this, you immediately turn away to give the impression that you have no knowledge of any of the actions your spectators have taken or will take. You double the sum you have learned (2 times 30 is 60), and the result is what you predict—60. Be certain to hand your prediction to one of the spectators before going further, and impress this on everyone. Then proceed, as above, and you will end with a surprising climax.

The principle is similar to that used in Date Choice, but with Date Choice you have to make a plus or minus adjustment for the various days chosen. In Stover's Prediction you are automatically forcing the values of either diagonal line—or the equivalent of a diagonal line—of values. (Note that each diagonal will total 60.) Your spectator self-forces upon himself the equivalent of one of the diagonals by virtue of the procedures.

The clever mathematician-magician, Stewart James, worked out a variation of this using anagram cards (cards bearing letters of the alphabet). These cards are used in various spelling and mental effects. The following uses James' application, but applied with regular playing cards. (This is being included in the "Calendar Magic" chapter because of its similarity to Stover's Prediction.)

Let us assume that you knew 1945 was a year with a significant meaning to a friend. Perhaps this is the anniversary date of your friend, or the year in which his first child was born, or had some other personal value. You would secretly arrange a deck of cards placing the four aces on top, under them you place the four 9's, under these cards you place the four 4's, and lastly the four 5's. Thus, from the top down you would have four aces (1's), followed by the four 9's, the four 4's, the four 5's, and then the remainder of the deck. Place the deck in its case. When ready to perform, remove the deck from the case and riffle shuffle without disturbing the top 16 cards. Deal the top four cards face down in a row, and to the right of them deal the next four cards, and continue until you have dealt four rows of four cards, as shown below:

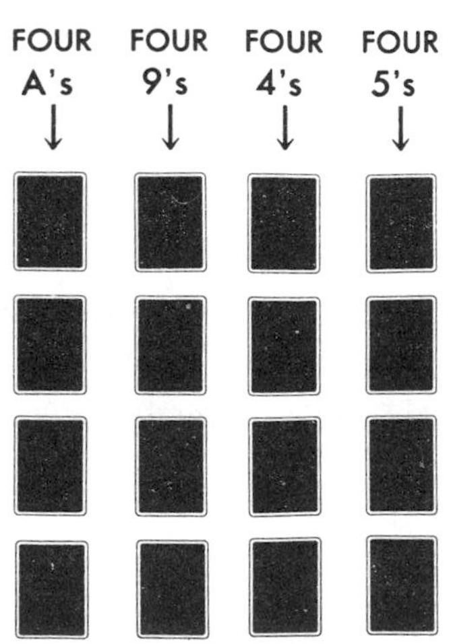

You now lead the conversation along the lines of the date you are now going to "force." You could say, "You know, there is an unusual relationship between events that have occurred and a deck of cards. For example, a deck contains 52 cards, just as our calendars have 52 weeks. There are four suits, and our calendars are divided into four seasons. There are 13 cards in a suit and the calendar actually consists of 13 four week months. I've dealt some cards on the table to test this relationship. I want you to go back say fifteen or twenty years. For example, think of some year during the 1940's that was particularly important to you. Something very close to you that happened in the early forties." This line of conversation will lead your spectator to the year which you are set for.

You now request that he touch the back of any of the 16 cards. Have him place a coin on the card touched. You now request that he hand you all of the cards which are directly above or below the card he has chosen, and also all of the cards which are either to the left or the right of his selection. (As these cards are handed to you simply cut them into the center of the deck.) This procedure is continued until only four cards remain on the table. (This has actually been a self-force of one card of each row and line, similar to the diagonal relationship attained in Stover's Prediction!)

To conclude, pick up the four remaining cards, have your spectator name the year he has "selected," and arrange the four cards to form 1945. If presented correctly, this demonstration can be more effective than many items requiring a good deal more work on your part.

(9) any day called for

Although seldom performed, this is an interesting calendar stunt that requires a minimum of effort. Upon being given any date, for example, August 4th, 1856, you can immediately name what day of the week this date occurred.

There are many methods for performing this, but that described by the late Royal V. Heath (a most original performer in the mathematical-magic field) is quite efficient.

You require the three tables, as given below. I suggest that you make these up by copying them on business cards. They will thus take little space and always be available for your demonstration of this stunt.

TABLE A

	Add	
January	1	*(Add 0 if a leap year)*
February	4	*(Add 3 if a leap year)*
March	4	
April	0	
May	2	
June	5	
July	0	
August	3	
September	6	
October	1	
November	4	
December	6	

TABLE B	*Add*
1900–2000	0
1800–1900	2
1752–1800 (9/14)	4
1700–1752 (9/2)	1
1600–1700	2

Add 1 for each century earlier

TABLE C

Sunday	Monday	Tuesday	Wednesday	Thursday	Friday	Saturday
1	2	3	4	5	6	0

Let us use August 4th, 1856 as our first example. Perform the following steps:

(a) Use the last two digits of the year, in this case, 56. Divide 4 into this number (disregarding any remainder), and add the result to the original two digits. Thus, 56 divided by 4 results in 14; and 14 plus 56 is 70, which is our working number.

(b) Add the month number as indicated in Table A. Referring to Table A we find that we must add 3 for August. Thus, 70 plus 3 gives us 73 as our working number.

(c) Add the value of the day. In this example, we must add 4 to 73, for a new working number of 77.

(d) Add the year number as indicated in Table B. Referring to Table

B we find that since the year fell between the 1800–1900 group we must add 2 to our working number, giving us a new working number of 79.

(e) Divide 7 into the final total. *Note:* We are now concerned with any remainder. After the division, if there is no remainder then, upon referring to Table C, we know that the day in question fell on a Saturday. If there is a remainder, we must refer to Table C to learn which day is involved. Let us take our working number, 79, and divide it by 7. We find that 7 goes into 79 eleven times with a remainder of 2. By referring to Table C we find that 2 indicates Monday. We therefore know that August 4th, 1856 occurred on a Monday!

As another example let us take the date December 26, 1962.

(a) 62 divided by 4 is 15 (ignoring any remainder). 62 plus 15 is 77, our present working number.

(b) Referring to Table A we must add to our total 6, as we are working with the month of December. Our working total is now 83 (77 plus 6).

(c) We must now add the value of the day, 26, to our working total: 83 plus 26 equals our new working total: 109.

(d) Refer to Table B to add in the year number. We find that 0 is added in for this group, thus our working total remains at 109.

(e) We now divide 109 by 7. Our result is 15, with a remainder of 4. Referring to Table C we find that 4 indicates December 26th, 1962, occurred on a Wednesday.

Carry the tables with you but don't let your spectators see you refer to them. In this way you will be given credit for a prodigious memory!

Chapter 4

mental magic

Many of the applications in this book suggest that you present the item as a mind-reading feat or another form of mentalism (prediction, thought transference, etc.). The reason for this is that in many of the effects you secure a certain amount of information, which appears to be of *limited* value, but which actually is the essentials to help you determine the figures your spectator started with or will ultimately arrive at. To simply state that "I now know you started with number 34," or another blunt remark is much too direct and immediately suggests that some simple computation on your part has led you to the necessary information. Thus, I have suggested the guise of mentalism not only as a form of intentional misdirection (on the thought processes of your spectators) but also as a medium for an entertaining presentation.

The applications of the mathematical principles discussed in this chapter are more pointedly aimed at mentalism. With the constant flow of publicity regarding mind-reading, Extra Sensory Perception, and other forms of mentalism there is an astonishing interest in the subject. Many believe that transference of thought is man's sixth sense—a delicate and still undeveloped sense, but nonetheless, a potential which someday will be within the ability of everyone. Speaking from my own years of experience in this general field, I can state that there *may be* the possibility of true thought transference, but

I have never witnessed any exhibition that I would consider as true evidence.

Many people, usually in totally unrelated fields, point to the work of Dr. Rhine of Duke University, and on the basis of Dr. Rhine's experiments, accept the plausibility and incidence of thought transference. Many of Dr. Rhine's conclusions are based upon mathematical probabilities. One of the tests most popularly used by Dr. Rhine is to have subject A handle a shuffled packet of special symbol cards and turn one face up, concentrating upon the symbol which appears on the card he is handling. His object is to transfer his impression of this symbol to subject B, who could be in another room, another city, or another country for that matter. Subject B attempts to receive A's impression, and writes down the impression he has received. A then looks at the next symbol card, attempting to send this impression to B. B, again, records the impression he has received, and this process is continued until the run of cards has been exhausted. The order of the cards A "sent" is then checked against the impressions which B has "received."

In these experiments, Dr. Rhine uses the 5 symbols pictured below:

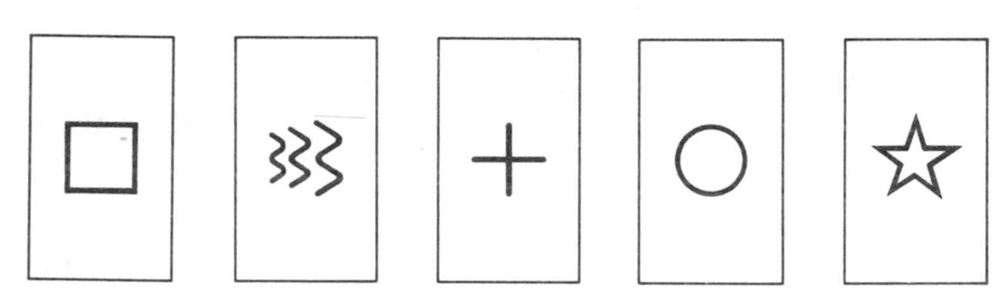

These symbols are repeated 5 times each so that a typical packet would consist of 25 of these cards. With 5 symbols repeated 5 times each, the chance results (pure guesswork) is to name 5 correct out of 25 attempts. As Dr. Rhine analyzes it, if two subjects start to hit a percentage greater than pure chance (more than 5 out of 25 correctly) he suspects that there may be thought transference involved. (If subjects hit below the probability average he then believes that these people may have no E. S. P. potential, or they are E. S. P. negatives.) Of course, as the word implies, probabilities are the expected results under certain conditions and circumstances. Probabilities does not mean that, since the chances are 1 out of 5, or 5 out of 25, the results will follow this expected pattern *exactly*. In fact, if the probability of a run of symbol cards is 5 out of 25, and if 5 out of 25 was exactly and consistently hit over a large number of runs, this in itself would be a near mathematical miracle!

Thus, probabilities is the expected potential. There will be various "runs" of greater or lesser incidence. But it is almost absurd to expect an exact conformation to the chance results. For example, we know that when tossing a coin in the air it can fall either heads up or tails. Thus, in every two tosses the probability is that one should be heads and the other tails . . . if we follow Rhine's reasoning. (Actually, the probability is 50–50 that a particular side will fall, and this percentage stands up *before* every toss and regardless of what tosses or runs have previously occurred.)

It is obvious that to expect a consistent run of one head and one tail *every* two tosses is just about impossible to anticipate. Various runs will evolve, in an unexpected pattern. Thus, how can a run, or incidence of greater than the expected probability, be accepted as proof of E. S. P.? Actually, long runs or hits are usually compensated for by runs which show below anticipated results.

This digression is given to extend some background in the field of E. S. P. This is the one field of mentalism that has been approached under scientific, though mathematically misguided, conditions.

The various effects discussed in this chapter should be presented as entertainment, not as serious explorations into this still undeveloped field. The first item is a most interesting application of mathematics to a mental effect.

(1) variation on a theme

Jack Yates, a clever English mathematician-magician, applied what is basically a computation effect to create a mental trick. I've carried the effect further than did Yates, and added a "kicker" to the original presentation.

Ask your spectators to remove three objects (or more, if you wish) from their pockets and place them on a table. Any three objects may be used, but you secretly determine if the chosen objects spell with a different number of letters.

For example, let us assume that one spectator removes a dime (spells with 4 letters), another a watch (spells with 5 letters), and another a wallet (spells with 6 letters). This would be an ideal group of objects, all spelling with a different number of letters, and so you would simply continue with the effect.

Let us assume that one removes a coin, and another a ring. Since both objects spell with the same number of letters (4), you would have to eliminate one of the objects. You could eliminate the dime, for example, by saying, "Let's leave money out of this. Could you please bring out another object." A key (3 letters), cigarette (9 letters), or other object can easily be substituted.

Let us assume that a dime, watch, and wallet have been removed. At this point (since you can continue with these items) you turn away from your spectators and proceed with the effect.

Request that one of your spectators mentally choose one of the objects. (Let us assume that he decides to think of the watch.)

Tell him to think of the object, and to mentally spell the name of the object he is thinking of. He is asked to count the letters which are in the name of the object. (In this example, he would spell w-a-t-c-h to himself, and ascertain that there are 5 letters in the name.)

"I want you to multiply the number of letters you are thinking of by 5," you next instruct the spectator. (He will multiply 5 by 5 for a product of 25.)

Your next remark is: "I've only attempted this mental test 3 times before, so will you please add three to the total you are now thinking of." (Spectator adds 3 to 25, for a new total of 28.)

Your next instruction is for the spectator to double the total he is now thinking of. (28 doubled equals 56.)

Your final instruction is to have another spectator think of any digit between 1 and 9. He is told to whisper this to the spectator who is thinking of the mentally chosen object, and this number is to be added to the total. Let us assume that a spectator chooses the digit 7, and whispers this to the party who has been performing the various computations. (Thus, 7 is added to 56 for a final total of 63.)

"A total has been reached which could have no relation to the mentally chosen object, is that correct?" you ask. You request that this total be named. In this case you will be given the number 63.

This is all the information you require to not only name the mentally chosen object, but also to name the freely chosen digit! Your work is quite simple. You need merely to mentally subtract 6 from the total named. In this case, 6 from 63 leaves a remainder of 57. The digit to the left, the 5, indicates the number of *letters* in the name of the mentally chosen object; the digit to the right, the 7, indicates the mentally chosen number.

To conclude the effect, face your spectators and glance at the objects. You can quickly determine which object spells with 5 letters. Of course, in this case, it is the watch. Go through the process of reading the spectator's mind and finally inform him that you receive an impression of a dial . . . and ticking . . . thus, it must be the watch. Very casually say, "Incidentally, did one of you think of a number?" Upon receiving an affirmative reply ask the spectator who thought of the number to concentrate upon it. Build this up, and finally disclose that "I get a strong flash of the number 7!" This "kicker" will prove quite effective.

You had the spectator add 3 to his early computation. To find the two essential numbers you always double the value of the number you give to the spectator (2 times 3 equals 6) and you subtract this doubled value from the total given to you. If, instead of 3, you had asked your spectator to add in 8, you would have had to subtract 16 (2 times 8) from the final total to determine the object-number and the thought of number. To show how this works, let us use the same figures for the spectators but change the number you suggest to 8. The watch is thought of (5 letters) and this is multiplied by 5 for a product of 25. To this you have him add 8, for a new total of 33. He next doubles this, bringing the working total to 66. The mentally thought of number, 7, is now added to the total for a final sum of 73. Upon being given the total 73 you simply subtract 16, and your result is 57, which gives you the necessary information.

The process of multiplying a number by 5 and then doubling the result is a series which merely results in the multiplication of the original number by 10. Example, using watch (5 letters), 5 times 5 equals 25. If 25 is now doubled, it brings the total to 50, which is actually 10 times 5. However, by having the performer's number added in *before* the doubling process, you conceal this. Example, 5 times 5 is 25, plus 3 is 28, and doubled is 56. If you were given the total 56 at this point, the method might be obvious. However, by having a mentally chosen number added to the total (in our example, 7), the total 63 appears completely unrelated to any of the numbers worked with.

When you are given this total you must remove your original number (3) which has been doubled, advancing it to 6, to get to your informative number. 6 from 63 is 57, which is 10 times the original number (5), plus the mentally chosen number (7) which was added in.

As suggested above, as many objects may be used as you wish, the only reservation being that you check to make sure that they spell with a different number of letters.

(2) hand-writing divination

Many people believe in divination through the use of inanimate objects. For example, a fortune teller's crystal ball. Centuries ago the magician's wand was considered as a source of unusual power. Along these general lines, you can perform an interesting test among a group of people.

In essence, you borrow a sheet of paper and tear it into 8 slips, handing 4 of the slips to ladies, and the other 4 to gentlemen. You now turn away from the group and request that each write upon his slip a number that has some personal meaning. For example, a number representing a birthday, a telephone number, an address or some other bit of information which you could not know of or relate to any of the people writing.

The slips are collected and mixed before you turn and again face the spectators. "Each has written a number on his slip of paper. Now, quite frankly, it is impossible for me to directly relate what has been written on each slip with the person who has done the writing. Nor can I identify the person, since I am not familiar with your various styles of handwriting. However, I can divine the sex of the person who has done the writing just by concentrating upon each slip. As I look at the slips I would appreciate it if you each concentrate upon what you have written. I will try and receive an impression for each of you."

You pick the slips up, one at a time, and after a few moments of concentration you infallibly state the sex of the person whose slip you are holding. For example, you could have a slip in front of you that bore the number 7342. You might say something along these lines: "I have a slip with the number 7342 written on it. Who ever wrote that please concentrate. I think I'm getting it. Yes, yes . . . a lady! Who wrote this please?" and the lady who wrote this will identify herself.

This is an off-beat presentation which will prove of great interest and earn you credit for either receiving an impression from each of the people or for expert hand-writing analysis.

The method for performing this is well concealed behind the presentation. Mathematically speaking, the method is in the manner in which you tear the paper, when you divide the sheet into 8 slips (or pieces). You tear the sheet of paper as follows:

(a) Fold the paper along its long center, as pictured below, and tear it into two equal pieces, placing X behind Y.

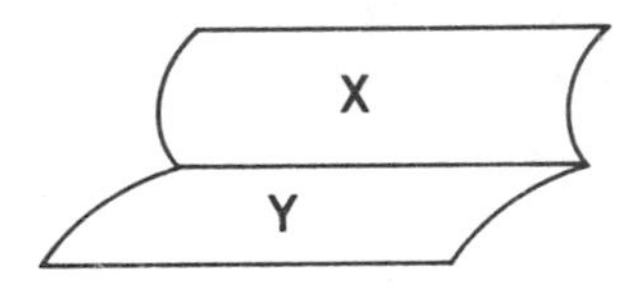

(b) You must now tear this double strip at three points to result in 8 fairly equal slips. To do this you must make the tears at T-1, T-2, and T-3, as indicated below:

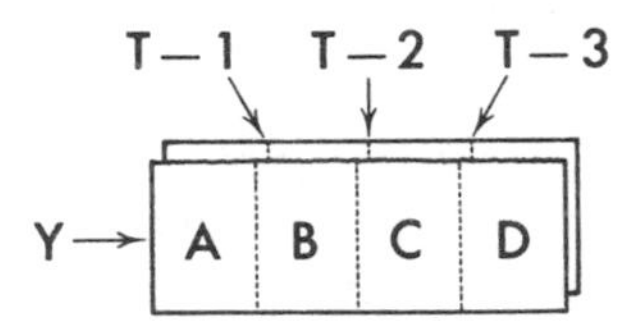

(c) Make the first tear at T-1 and place A pair on top of the B section.

(d) Make your second tear at T-2, placing A and B pairs on top of section C.

(e) You make your last tear at T-3, but place the D pair on top of the other three pairs. (This will be fully understood after a trial run.) Hand the first 4 slips (the top slips) to 4 ladies, and the remaining slips to 4 gentlemen. Your work has been completed, and you now turn away and have each spectator write a number upon his or her slip. You may suggest that each try to conceal his style of handwriting if he wishes. After the slips have been collected and mixed you face your spectators, look at each slip, and attempt to receive a thought impression from each spectator. Actually, as you look at each slip you simply note if it has two or three torn sides (or edges). If the slip you are looking at has two torn sides it will belong to one of the ladies; if it has three torn sides it will belong to a gentleman. Once you have your information, the rest is simply good acting.

The process by which you have torn the slips, as outlined in the above steps, results in the top 4 slips ending with two torn edges and the last 4 with three torn edges! Don't let the simplicity of this deter you from learning and doing a most entertaining stunt.

(3) think of a card

It would be difficult to complete this chapter without the inclusion of a version of the THINK OF A CARD computation effect. You may recall versions of this when you were a child, and you may also remember the fun you had with it.

In brief, someone thinks of a card, performs a few computations, and you determine the thought-of card after learning the result of the computations.

Let us assume that your spectator mentally selected the 8 of Spades. Of course, at this point you don't know the card he is thinking of. You have him perform the following computations:

(a) Add the next highest value to the one you are thinking of. (In this case, your spectator would add 9 to the value 8, for a working total of 17.)

(b) Multiply your present total by 5. (Your spectator would multiply 17 by 5, for a new working total of 85.)

(c) Your spectator must now add to this total a value to represent the suit of the card he has selected. He is requested to add 1 to the number he is working with if the card he mentally chose was a Club, 2 if a Diamond, 3 if a Spade, and 4 if a Heart. (Since he actually thought of a Spade he would add 3 to 85 for a final total of 88.)

(d) You request that this final total be given to you. As soon as you learn this, (in this case, 88), you can easily name the mentally selected card. To determine the thought-of card you simply deduct 5 from the final total. In this case, 5 is deducted from 88, for a remainder of 83. The digit to the left, the 8, indicates the value of the mentally chosen card. The digit to the right, the 3, indicates the suit of the card. Referring to step "c" you know that 3 is representative of the Spade suit. Thus, you know that the thought-of card was the 8 of Spades.

The mechanics of this is similar to the method used in Variation On a Theme. When the spectator adds "the next highest value" to his original value he is actually doubling his mentally chosen number, plus 1. Multiplying this by 5 results in the original value being multiplied by 10, plus the single digit (the 1) being multiplied by 5. Note that the result in step "b" is actually this: 10 times the original value (8) plus 5.

Step "c" results in the addition of a value representative of the suit. When you deduct 5 from the final total you are left with 10 times the original value, plus a digit (value) representative of the selected suit.

You can have several people perform the computations simultaneously, each using a card he has mentally selected. Ask each for his final total, subtract 5 from each total given to you, and you can immediately name the card each has chosen. (Note: a jack would be given the value of 11, a queen 12, and a king 13.)

(4) canar's think of a card

The previously described method, and similar methods for performing this stunt, all follow the same approach. The late Harry Canar, a West Coast magician, developed an interesting variation to this effect which, to my knowledge, is little known. It has several intriguing elements which will tend to "throw off" those familiar with the more conventional approaches to this problem.

Again, a card is mentally chosen, but since a few additional computations must be performed, the spectator is given a slip of paper to work with. Let us assume that the selected card is the 7 of Spades. Of course, you would not know the value and suit of the mentally chosen card.

The procedure is as follows:

(a) The value of the selected card is written on the slip of paper. In this case, your spectator would write the digit 7.

(b) Anyone from the audience is now invited to call out any number from 1 to 25, and your spectator is requested to add this number to the value of the card he has chosen. Let us assume that someone calls out the number 17. Your spectator adds this to his mentally chosen value (7) for a total of 24.

(c) You request that this new total be multiplied by 10. (24 times 10 is 240.)

(d) Your spectator is requested to add 1 to his total if the suit he has selected is a Club, 2 if a Heart, 3 if a Spade, and 4 if a Diamond. Since the chosen card was a Spade your spectator will add 3 to his total for a new total of 243.

(e) Anyone in the audience is now requested to call out another number, however this time the choice is confined to values between 25 and 85. Your spectator is asked to add this number to his secret total. Let us assume that the number now named is 37. Thus, your spectator would add 37 to 243 for a final total of 280.

(f) You now request that the spectator give you the final total. Upon learning this total you immediately name the mentally chosen card.

You must perform a few simple operations, during the course of this stunt, to be able to determine the mentally chosen card. Your first step is to note the value of the *first* number named by one of the audience, and multiply this by 10. In this case, the first number named was a 17, so you mentally multiply this by 10 and remember 170 as your "working key" number. Your second step is to note the *second* number named by one of the audience, and add this to your "working key" number. In this case, 37 was the second number. You would thus mentally add 37 to 170, for a "key" of 207.

Upon learning your spectator's final total, in this case 280, you subtract your "key" from it. 207 subtracted from 280 leaves a remainder of 73. The digit to the left, the 7, indicates the value of the mentally chosen card; and the digit to the right, the 3, is representative of the suit of the card.

You simply convert this number, the 3, back into its suit value. In this case, it would be returned to its suit: Spades, and you would thus know that your spectator mentally selected the 7 of Spades. Of course, as in the first THINK OF A CARD method, if the digit to the right was a 1 it would indicate that the selected suit was a Club, if it had been a 2 it would have indicated a Heart, etc.

Of course, the bare bones of the method in Canar's approach follows that of the initially described method. However, the addition of the two numbers which people in the audience name acts as excellent camouflage. Your secret computations result in the eventual subtraction of the "excess baggage" your spectator has added to his original starting figures.

(5) red, white, and blue

This is a classic mathematical-mental effect that is all too rarely performed. The method given here is quite simple and takes all the work out of what was once a more involved feat.

The performer hands a card to each of three spectators. The cards have various instructions on them, and appear as follows:

A	B	C
If you have the RED chip take	If you have the RED chip take	If you have the RED chip take
1 CARD	2 CARDS	4 CARDS
If you have the WHITE chip take	If you have the WHITE chip take	If you have the WHITE chip take
2 CARDS	4 CARDS	8 CARDS
If you have the BLUE chip take	If you have the BLUE chip take	If you have the BLUE chip take
3 CARDS	6 CARDS	12 CARDS

You remove three poker chips (or colored discs, if you wish) from your pocket and place them on the table. One chip is red, the second is white, and the third chip is blue. You also remove a group of blank cards from your wallet and place them on the table. (These "blank" cards may be business cards.)

You now turn your back to the three spectators and request that each choose whichever chip he wishes and have the chips concealed on the person of each spectator so that it is impossible for you to know which spectator has selected which chip. While you are turned away each of your three spectators is told to follow the instructions that appear on his particular card.

Upon the completion of the above tasks you face your spectators and immediately divine the correct color of the chip each has concealed on his person!

You apparently have no information, yet you can perform this without fail.

You require three different colored chips (or colored discs), three instruction cards as shown above, 17 blank cards (or business cards), and a small card with the information on it as depicted below:

0— RWB
1— WRB
2— RBW
4— BRW
5— WBR
6— BWR

The poker chips and instruction cards can be carried in your jacket pockets. The 17 blank (or business) cards should be in your wallet in a convenient location. For purposes of deception carry only the 17 cards so that when you decide to show this stunt you need simply remove ALL of the cards in a group stating, "We will need some cards for this. Here, these will do." In this way it will appear that a random number of cards have been removed. To have to count out a specific number of cards in front of your spectators will suggest your working method.

The small card should be typed or written in small and neat letters. The best spot for it is under a celluloid partition in your wallet so that you can easily refer to it upon taking out your wallet and opening it for the removal of a bill.

The method depends upon the fact that after the instructions are carried out by your three spectators there are only six amounts of blank cards which will remain: none (0), 1, 2, 4, 5, or 6. The permutations are as follows: since three spectators may perform one of three acts, the possibilities are $1 \times 2 \times 3$, or a total of 6 possibilities.

To perform, you must give instruction card A to the spectator to your left, card B to the one in the center, and card C to the spectator to your right. It is essential that they be given out in this order.

After you have distributed the instruction cards, turn away from your spectators. Have each choose one of the poker chips and hide them from your view. Then have each carry out the instructions which are on his card. Each is to conceal the blank cards he removes from the group.

After this has been done, you turn towards your spectators. You must now note if there are any blank cards remaining on the table, and if so, how many. If there are some cards remaining the best way to get a count on them is to push them aside, spreading them as you do so. In this way you can easily determine the amount remaining without obviously counting them. As you push the cards aside you say, "We no longer need these."

Let us assume that you have noted 4 cards remained on the table after the completion of the instructions. Remember the number 4.

Mention that each has freely chosen a poker chip and that it is impossible for you to know who has which particular chip. Request that each concentrate on the color of the chip he is concealing.

Remove your wallet and open it to remove a bill. As you open your wallet quickly glance at the card under the celluloid and note what is written after the number 4. In this case, you would see the letters BRW. In a continuous gesture remove one of your bills and say, "I am willing to bet this amount that I have read your minds and I can tell you what colored chip each of you has." Of course, this is a ruse to assist you in gaining the necessary information: BRW.

BRW indicates that the spectator to your left has the blue (B) chip in his pocket, the spectator in the center has the red (R) chip hidden from view, and the spectator to your right has the white (W) chip concealed.

If 2 blank cards remained, after the completion of the following of the instructions, you would have noted the initials RBW next to 2 in your wallet. In this case, the person to your left would have the red (R) chip, the one in the center would have the blue (B) chip, and the last spectator would have the white (W) chip.

The working should now be clear; there are only six possibilities, and each of the combinations of the possibilities are listed on the card in your wallet.

(6) the book test

One of the most impressive tests a mentalist can perform is that of apparently having someone select a word, from a borrowed book or magazine, which the mentalist (after due concentration) names. The method described here does not infringe upon the excellent machinations utilized by the more sophisticated professional, but it will enable you to perform an excellent copy of the general effect . . . and under unprepared circumstances.

The little details involved in working towards the climax of this and other effects should be submerged in the presentation. Your spectators should remember only the direct effect: that you have read a mind, or divined a thought—not the building blocks which appear to be of little consequence, but the absence of which would leave you helpless.

Can you conceive of a method for accomplishing the following: You are at a friend's home. You borrow a book or magazine that you plan to use in a mental test. You tell your spectators that a page and a word will be selected under conditions which are beyond reproach. "To afford a completely chance selection," you say, "I would like someone to remove the number or digit cards from a borrowed pack. To make it fairly representative, please remove the ace to nine of any suit." The cards are to represent numbers, the ace being 1, the deuce 2, and so on so that the nine cards can obviously be formed into endless combinations. The cards are mixed and dealt face down on the table. A spectator freely chooses several of the cards. You say, "Please add the value of the cards you have selected. For example, if you find the cards add to 22 then please turn to page 22 in the borrowed book. To choose a word please add the digits together. For example, using 22 as your total, you would add 2 plus 2 together, for a sum of 4. Thus, you would look at the 4th word on page 22 and concentrate on it. If, for example, the sum of the cards adds to 14 you would then turn to page 14 in the book and look at the 5th word, the digit 1 and the digit 4 adding to 5." Your spectator adds the value of the cards together, turns to the page in the book corresponding to this total, and looks at the word that is the sum of the digits. Upon due concentration, you name the word your spectator is thinking of!

Now the above is a fairly accurate description of the effect . . . as far as your spectators are concerned. If performed with ease, they will only remember the direct effect: You named a word they thought of. They will forget or submerge the "little details" which resulted in the choice of the particular page and word they arrived at.

Actually, this is a clever mathematical force of the page and word. To perform, you must first borrow a book or magazine. (If a magazine is used, you may find that the particular page involved may have an illustration or advertisement. In this situation, you would describe what was on the page—via your spectators' thoughts [?], rather than a selected word.) Let us assume that you have been handed a book. Mention that you have never seen this before, and as you handle the book thumb through it as if simply giving it a perfunctory examination. Actually, open it to page 15 and look at and memorize the 6th word on this page. Let us assume that the word is: speak.

To your spectators it should appear as if you have done nothing more than flipped through the book. Actually, you have secured all of the information you will require.

After you have the vital information (in this case, the word "speak") place the book down. Borrow a deck of playing cards and discuss the fact that you want a free choice of a page and a word made in the book the spectator has chosen to use. Request that someone remove all of the digit cards of any one particular suit. Point out that by using the ace to 9 of a suit gives you nine digits to work with, and that these digits can form and be formed into an endless number of combinations. After the nine cards have been removed set them up, to check that they are all there, by setting them so that they run 1 (ace), 2, 3, etc. through to 9. The 1 should be on the top of the packet and the 9 on the bottom if the cards were squared and turned face downwards.

Turn the cards face down and state that you are going to mix them. You apparently do mix them in a random manner, but by following the next instructions very closely your mix (or shuffle) will actually return the cards to the original 1 to 9 starting position. To perform this "mix" hold the cards face down in your left hand in usual dealing fashion. With your left thumb push the cards to the right so that three of them can be taken onto the palm of your right hand. Push three more from your left hand into your right hand, but take these *on top* of the original three cards which were dealt into your right hand. Place the remaining cards in your left hand *under* the six cards now held in your right hand. Take the entire packet of nine cards back into your left hand, and duplicate the above steps. The packet will once again run, from top down, 1 to 9. Performed rapidly, the above sequence will give the impression of a random mixing of the cards. Repeat the above two phases a few times and your spectators will accept the fact that they are mixed hopelessly.

Deal the top card onto the table, the second card to the right of it, and continue dealing until you have dealt out the top five cards, as shown below:

You have dealt the top five cards from left to right. Continue dealing, but this time from right to left, by dealing the sixth card on top of the fourth card dealt, the seventh card on top of the third card dealt, the next card on top of the second card dealt, and the last card on top of the first card dealt. You will have four pairs of cards, from left to right, and one single card to the right of the four pairs:

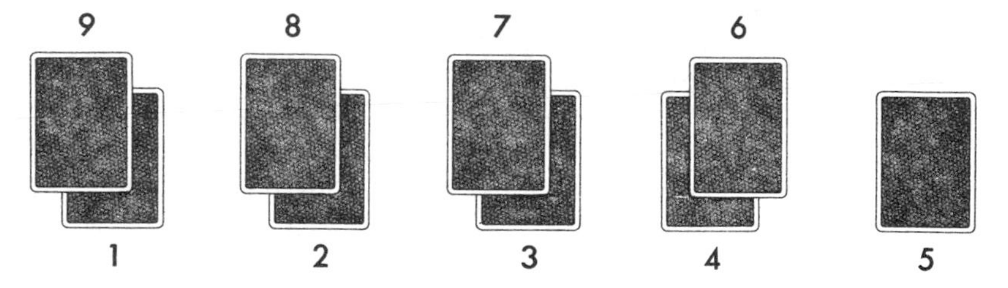

Since the cards were apparently mixed, and they are face down, this haphazard pattern of dealing will leave your spectators with no idea as to the location of any of the cards.

Mention that you have one odd card, and hand this card (face down) to one of the spectators. Say, "I'd like you to drop this on any one of the pairs. Make a free choice, please, and whichever pair you drop it on you will use." Your spectator follows your instructions, and as soon as he has selected a pair you scoop up the other three pairs and return them to the deck.

You now proceed as earlier in the description of this test by having your spectator pick up the three cards he has "selected" and have him add the values together to arrive at a page selection. (The three cards will always add to 15.) Request that the digits be added together (1 plus 5 equals 6) and request that he look at the word indicated by this latter sum. Of course, your spectator will find that the word he looks at is "speak," which you have conveniently memorized.

Add some drama in disclosing the word. For example, have your spectator think of the word and say, "I can't get too clear an impression. Wait . . . wait! I get the letter 's' and a 'b' . . . no it's a 'p' . . . I think I have it. Sp—, Speak! Is that the word?"

Needless to say, as a little investigation will show you, your spectator can only arrive at a total of 15 by virtue of the manner in which the cards have been placed down. Thus, by learning the 6th word on the 15th page of any book or magazine you are prepared for the performance of a most effective mental test.

A little homework and you can work out various other combinations. For example, with a total of 15 you can have your spectators transpose the digits (make them into 51 instead of 15) and turn to page 51 if they wish. If you do this you simply prepare for this eventuality by taking the trouble to note the 6th word on the 51st page *as well as* the 6th word on the 15th page. You can thus offer your spectators a greater range of choice and still bring the effect off.

(7) hummer's three object divination

One of the truly inventive minds in mathematical magic is Bob Hummer's. Many individuals have developed ingenious solutions to problems or fascinating methods, but Hummer's brilliance is in the creation of effects.

Hummer's Three Object Divination is a most delightful application of logic to a divination effect.

Three objects are borrowed and placed on a table. Let us assume that they are a ring, a coin, and a watch. Assume that the ring is to the left, which will be known as position 1; the coin is in the center, which will be known as position 2; and the watch is to the right of the other objects, which will be known as position 3, (fig. 1):

Fig. 1

You say the following, "When I turn my back I am going to have you exchange or switch places with any two of the objects. Now it doesn't matter which objects you exchange, but I want you simply to tell me the two positions which are involved. For example, let us assume that you change the places of the ring and coin. You would simply say to me: '1 and 2' and nothing more." You actually make the exchange in front of your spectators, (fig. 2), so that they will understand how to proceed.

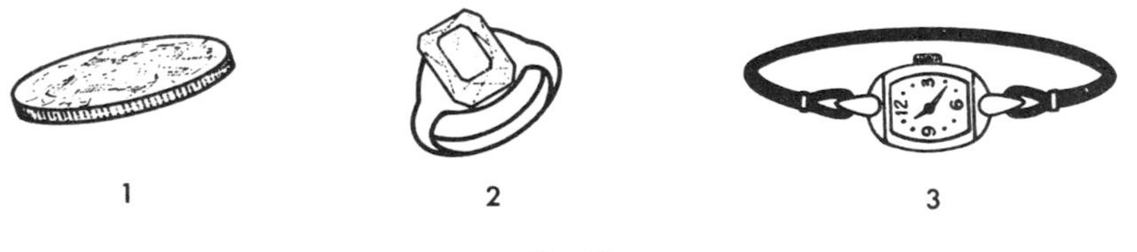

Fig. 2

"I will now turn my back so I can't see the objects you exchange. I am going to have you make as many exchanges as you wish, however, every time you make an exchange you simply call out the positions involved."

At this point, you turn away from the objects so that you can't see which objects are handled. Your spectator starts to exchange objects, calling out the positions, and he may do so as many times as he wishes and as rapidly as he wishes. For example, you might hear the following from your spectator: "1 and 3 . . . 2 and 3 . . . 2 and 1 . . . etc."

After he is satisfied that the objects have been well mixed you request that he think of any one of the objects. He is now told to secretly exchange the other two objects—neither of which has been thought of, to "throw me off the scent." He does *not* call the positions on this exchange.

After this has been done, he is once again instructed to make as many more exchanges as he wishes, but he is again to call the positions involved as he did in the first phase of this effect.

After your spectator has made as many additional exchanges as he wishes you turn towards him. Without asking any questions you request that he concentrate upon the mentally selected object. You immediately pick up the correct object and hand it to him!

Hummer uses simple logic, plus the use of your fingers as a recording device, to bring this test to a successful conclusion.

The method depends upon keeping track of the position of one of the objects. Let us assume that the objects are in position as in fig. 2 before you turn your back. And let us assume that you decide to keep track of the watch, which is in position 3. Turn your back, and bend your right fingers into a loose fist. Your thumb is going to be the marking device, and your first, second, and third fingers will respectively indicate position 1, position 2, and position 3. Thus, you would place your right thumb against your third finger to indicate that the object you will keep track of is now in position 3. Your spectator starts to make exchanges. Let us assume that his first call is "1 and 2." Since position 3 was not involved you make no move. The second exchange is "1 and 3." You now move your thumb to your first finger, since the object you are keeping track of has now been moved to position 1. The next call is, say, "2 and 3." You make no move with your thumb since position 1 was not involved. The next call is "1 and 2." You move your thumb to your second finger, since the object you are tracking is now in position 2.

You can continue this way with great ease, regardless of the number of calls made or the rapidity with which your spectator makes the calls.

The strong deception is that, after ten or twelve calls, without seeing the objects it is virtually impossible for anyone to keep track of *three* objects. However, using Hummer's method, it is elementary to follow the route of one object!

At this point, after your spectator has satisfied himself with enough calls, he is requested to mentally select one of the objects. He is next instructed to exchange the other two objects, but not to call out the positions of this exchange so that "I will be thrown off the scent."

After this secret exchange, your spectator proceeds to make additional exchanges by once again calling out the positions. And you continue to record the exchanges with your thumb and right fingers.

After your spectator has made enough additional calls you turn towards him to conclude the effect. Let us assume that, at this point, your thumb indicates position 3, and the objects are on the table as in fig. 1. You look at the objects and note what object is now at position 3. If it is the watch you immediately know that the watch is the mentally selected object. The logic behind this is that you have been keeping track of the watch during the various exchanges. Since it is in the position it should have been in *had it not been moved* during the "secret" exchange, then it must be the chosen object. (The other two objects were "secretly" exchanged . . . the unselected objects.)

Let us assume that another object is in position 3, for example, the ring. You now know that this object was involved in the "secret" exchange since it (the ring) and the watch were the objects secretly exchanged. Thus, the only undisturbed object was the coin . . . and so the coin would be the mentally chosen object.

Once you try this you will be pleased with the effectiveness of this divination. There are many variations, but I would like to mention a simple idea I have added that can greatly add to the mystery. You borrow three objects, as in Hummer's original procedure, but you cover the objects by placing a cup over each object. Thus, the objects will be hidden from view. Go through the procedure of explaining how the exchanges and calls are to be made, but before you turn away from the table simply note what object is under the cup in the third position. Of course, the exchanges are made by switching the cups around from position to position, the objects sliding along under the cups. Let us assume that you have noted that the watch is in the third position before your spectator begins his calls. Simply "record" this by placing your right thumb on your third finger. Now turn away from the table and have your spectator make his various calls, keeping track of the location of the watch just as you did in the original description.

After several calls have been made tell your spectator to lift up one of the cups and think of the object that is under the cup he has elected to lift. Then tell him to make a secret exchange of the other two cups, without calling the positions. (Note: After several exchanges, your spectator will completely lose track of the location of the objects since they will also be hidden from his view!)

After the secret exchange, your spectator once again makes exchanges, and calls each exchange. Of course, when he resumes making calls you continue to keep track of the object you started with.

Let us assume that your spectator has been satisfied with his additional calls. Also, let us assume that, as you face your spectator and the three cups, your thumb indicates that the watch should be in position 2 (had it been undisturbed during the secret exchange).

Lift up the cup in position 2. If it is the watch immediately say, "This is the object you are thinking of." If the watch is not in position 2 you immediately say, "I know that this is not the object you are thinking of." Assuming the watch is not in position 2, request that your spectator place one of his hands on one of the mouth-down cups. Pick up the cup he has left free. If the watch is under it say, "I know that you did not think of this object. You had a strong impulse and your hand is now covering the object you thought of."

If the cup you lift reveals the object other than the watch, then you know that this is the mentally chosen object. You say, "I lifted a cup which I knew was not the object you thought of, and you covered a cup which did not hold the object you thought of . . . this is the object you thought of (indicating the object under the cup you have just lifted)."

As you can see, the use of the cups follows the same pattern and method as the original effect. However, the cups greatly add to the over-all effect. As you make your statements you must do so in a positive manner . . . as if you had planned all along to reveal the object, or eliminate the object you are dealing with. Just appear sure of yourself, so that each eventuality appears to be controlled by you, rather than the true reverse picture.

Chapter 5

magic squares

Known by mathematicians over 2,000 years ago, magic squares are a fascinating study. Basically, a magic square is an orderly arrangement of cells (or squares) which have numbers inscribed in each position. These numbers are so arranged that each line in the magic square, when added together, will equal the total of each other line. In addition, each row will have a similar total, as will the diagonals.

The basic nine-cell square below (fig. 1) will total 15 by adding the value of any of the lines, rows, or diagonals. In squares having a larger number of cells there can be many more relationships.

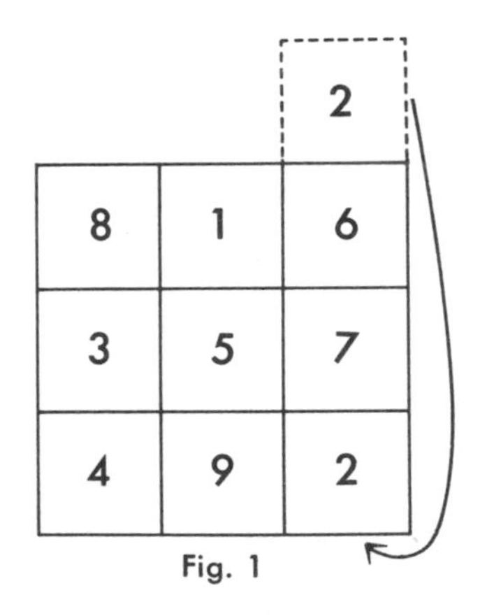

Fig. 1

Centuries ago many people thought that magic squares were invested with unusual powers. As a matter of fact, even to this day magic squares are impressed on small pieces of metal and worn as talismans by certain groups in India.

I must confess that I've never been a witness to any unusual powers inherent in magic squares, but they can be fun to construct and there are several amusing applications that can be demonstrated with them. Once you have an understanding of the methods of constructing various magic squares you will find them quite simple to produce.

There are endless methods and variations in constructing magic squares. Rather than get involved with transpositions, fractional squares, negative squares, squares of unusual shape, and the endless varieties, I will discuss a few of the more direct methods. Maurice Kraitcheck, in his book *Mathematical Recreations,* has covered much ground discussing many of the more complex and technically fascinating squares, should you be a more serious student of the subject.

(1) the basic square

The procedures for constructing the nine-cell square is applied to other odd-celled squares (25 cells, 49 cells, etc.). Let us assume that you wish to construct the nine-cell square as in fig. 1. You may begin with any number, but for the sake of simplicity let us use the number 1.

(a) After drawing a nine-cell blank, insert 1 in the center cell of the top line. You must visualize the top and bottom lines as being attached to each other, or as continuations of each other. You must also visualize the left and right rows as continuations of each other.

(b) Each consecutive number (in odd-celled magic squares) must be inserted in its cell by placing it one square to the right and one square above the previously placed number. This is an oblique movement. 2 can't be placed one to the right and one above its prior number as this would place it outside of the confines of the square, illustrated by the dotted area in fig. 1. However, since you have visualized the top and bottom lines as being attached to each other you can conform to the above rule by placing the 2 at the bottom right corner, fig. 1. (If the top and bottom lines were actually attached to each other this is the cell in which the 2 would be placed.)

(c) Moving the next number, 3, one up and one to the right, would place it outside of the square. But since the left row is a visualized continuation of the right row, it can be placed in position as shown in fig. 1.

(d) 4 can't be placed one above and one to the right as this position is occupied by 1, a number placed earlier. Whenever a cell is occupied by a number, you must simply drop one cell *below* its immediate predecessor. Thus, 4 would be placed under 3, as in fig. 1.

(e) 5 and 6 are easily placed, using the one above and one to the right rule.

(f) 7 can't be placed because it falls in a diagonal position where there is no continuation of a line or row. In this situation, the number is treated just as if its space had been occupied by a previously inserted number. Thus, 7 is placed *below* its previously placed number.

(g) 8 and 9 are placed following the above rules, and your finished square is as in fig. 2, pictured below. Note the arrows and other indications showing the various movements of the numbers to their proper cells.

This square can be used starting with any number. If you started with

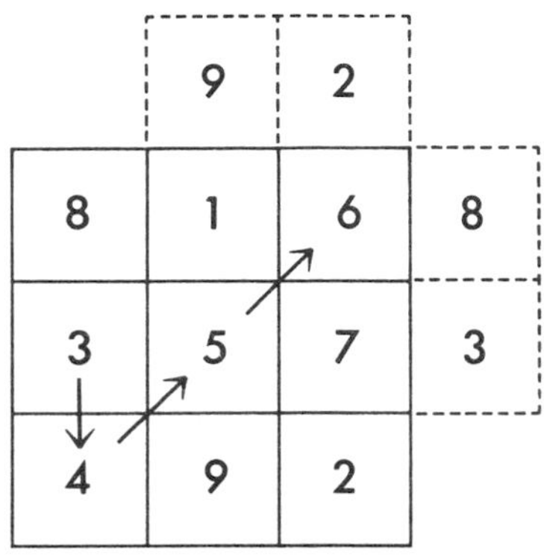

Fig. 2

2, for example, the square would advance to the "magic total" 18. Fig. 3 shows a nine-cell square starting with 2. Note that as you advance each number (at the start) the magic total advances by 3. Thus, a nine-cell square starting with 3 would render a magic total of 21, starting with 4 would bring the total to 24, etc.

9	2	7
4	6	8
5	10	3

Fig. 3

All odd-celled squares are formed following the same procedures as those just outlined for the nine-cell square. I will next describe a 25 cell square (five by five) so that you can note the identical procedures used for it and the nine-cell square.

(2) odd-cell squares

As in the nine-cell square, the first number must be placed in the center position of the first line. Below you will find an illustration of a 25 cell (five by five) magic square. For simplicity, this has been started with the number 1, but you may start with whatever value you wish. You follow the exact rules and procedures in completing this square as you did for the nine-cell square. Note that each line, row, and diagonal totals the same amount, in this case: 65. An additional magic total will be found by adding together the four corners plus the number in the exact center of the square (17–15–11–9 plus 13). Other more remote relationships may also be noted.

			2	
17	24	1	8	15
23	5	7	14	16
4	6	13	20	22
10	12	19	21	3
11	18	25	2	9

You may construct larger odd-cell squares by following the same procedures. These larger squares can become ungainly to handle and have little practical value other than to prove the range of the principles discussed.

(3) even-cell magic squares

An entirely different procedure is used for the construction of magic squares which have an even number of cells. Squares which are formed by multiples of four (16 cells, 64 cells, etc.) are all produced in similar fashion to the description given below. However, the 36 cell (six by six) square, although being an "even-celled magic square" is quite unique in itself.

I will discuss these various squares, but in actual practice you will find that the 16 cell and the 25 cell squares are the most popular. These are as impressive as larger squares and have the same interesting qualities, yet take less time to produce and are easier to prove out.

Let us start with the 16 cell square.

(a) After drawing a blank 16 cell square you must either draw in or visualize a line running across each diagonal. In the square below, note that two lines have been drawn in running from A to B and C to D. Let us start with the number 1 (of course, you may begin with any value you choose). You are going to fill in each number consecutively, starting with the upper left cell and working across to the right, with one reservation: Whenever you come to a square which is on a diagonal you will skip over this square. The 1 can't be placed in the upper left cell as it is on a diagonal. You therefore skip this cell, advance to the number 2 and place 2 in the second cell.

(b) The next number, 3, can be placed in its correct position, but 4 is on a diagonal and so must be skipped.

(c) 5 can be inserted in its correct cell, 6 and 7 are skipped, 8 is inserted, and you proceed to fill in all of the cells (skipping those on a diagonal) until you have run through the entire square. Your partially completed square will appear as follows:

A C

	2	3	
5			8
9			12
	14	15	

D B

(d) You must now fill in the open cells (those which were on a diagonal). Again, you start at the upper left cell, but instead of starting with the lowest number (in this case, number 1) and working forward you start with the highest number (in this case, 16) and count backwards. Insert 16 in the upper left cell. You count backwards, counting 15 for the next cell (which is occupied by 2), 14 for the next cell (which is occupied by 3), and 13 for the next cell. Since you reached an open cell, you fill 13 into this cell.

(e) Continuing the next line with 12 (occupied), you count backwards and fill in each open cell with the number that happens to fall when you hit each open position.

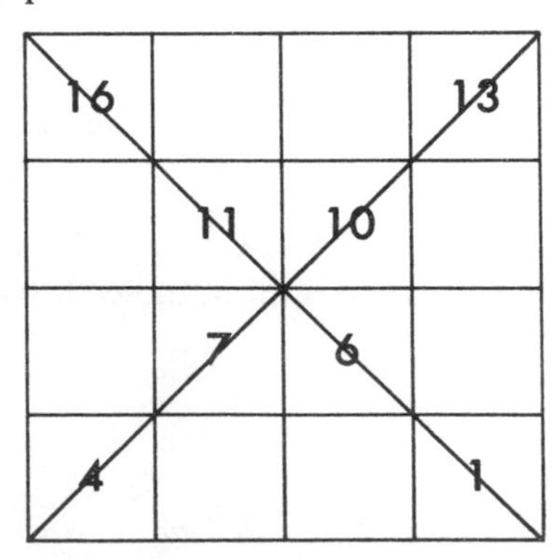

The above square indicates the completed backwards count, with all of the diagonal positions filled in. The completed magic square is shown below:

16	2	3	13
5	11	10	8
9	7	6	12
4	14	15	1

This particular square has a magic total of 34. Each line, row, and diagonal will add to 34. In addition, the four corners will also total 34 (16–13–4–1); the four center cells will total 34 (11–10–7–6); each corner group of four cells will total 34 (upper left: 16–2–11–5, lower left: 9–7–14–4, upper right: 3–13–8–10, lower right: 6–12–1–15); and, with some investigation, you will find additional groups which also relate to the magic total. As with all magic squares, any starting values may be used, which will of course change the magic totals. But the relationships will always be constant.

The 64-celled square (eight by eight) is constructed almost exactly as the square just described. The big difference is that in forming the 64-cell square you must set up the diagonals (or visualize them) on the basis of the large square consisting of four 16-celled squares. The square below shows the diagonal arrangement, and also the completed 64-celled square. Note that the same procedure applies to this large square as it did to the 16-celled square. When starting the "backward

64	2	3	61	60	6	7	57
9	55	54	12	13	51	50	16
17	47	46	20	21	43	42	24
40	26	27	37	36	30	31	33
32	34	35	29	28	38	39	25
41	23	22	44	45	19	18	48
49	15	14	52	53	11	10	56
8	58	59	5	4	62	63	1

count" you begin with 64, and continue backwards, filling in each cell falling on a diagonal.

Of course, in this large square you will find many inter-relationships due to the greater number of possibilities. For example, the lower right quarter of the 64-cell square consists of 16 cells which form a magic square totaling the magic total 130, with the exception of the diagonals. You can realize many unusual combinations should you investigate this further.

The 36-cell six by six square is actually a series of 4 nine-celled squares, plus a necessary transposition (exchange) of three numbers. Draw a 36-cell blank, but consider it as a structure of 4 nine-cell squares (note the heavy central intersecting lines). You actually fill it in by working on each nine-cell group as if it was a separate square and not as part of a larger structure.

(a) Begin filling in the upper left nine-cell group, just as you would a separate nine-celled square. Starting with number 1, place it in the center of the first line. The square below shows the completion of the upper left group.

8	1	6			
3	5	7			
4	9	2			

(b) Starting with the next consecutive number, in this case 10, fill in the lower right group of nine cells. The next square shows the completion of this stage.

8	1	6			
3	5	7			
4	9	2			
			17	10	15
			12	14	16
			13	18	11

(c) Starting with the next highest number, in this case 19, fill in the upper right group. After you have completed this, fill in the last remaining group (lower left). The square will appear as indicated below. Note, this is not the completed square as you must transpose three of the numbers.

8	1	6	26	19	24
3	5	7	21	23	25
4	9	2	22	27	20
35	28	33	17	10	15
30	32	34	12	14	16
31	36	29	13	18	11

(d) You must place numbers 8, 5, and 4 into the respective positions occupied by numbers 35, 32, and 31. This is indicated by the lines shown in the above square to point up these positions. The completed magic square, after the above transposition has been made, is shown below. Note that the lines, rows, and diagonals each add to 111. Also, the short-diagonals containing numbers 35–32–2 *plus* 33–5–4 add to 111, as does the short-diagonals containing numbers 24–23–22 *plus* 17–14–11. You can find many other relationships, some obvious and others quite remote.

35	1	6	26	19	24
3	32	7	21	23	25
31	9	2	22	27	20
8	28	33	17	10	15
30	5	34	12	14	16
4	36	29	13	18	11

(4) applications of standard magic squares

You are now in a position to produce magic squares of almost any size. Here is an excellent application, using 9-celled, 16-celled, or 25-celled magic squares.

Your spectator is requested to call out any two-digit number, for example, let us assume that he calls 27. You immediately write something on a slip of paper and hand it to someone for safe-keeping. You begin to produce a magic square, *starting* with the number the spectator has called.

After completing the square, and showing that the lines, rows, diagonals, etc. all add to the same magic total, you have an excellent punch-line to conclude with. Let us assume that the magic total is 93. You now request that the spectator who has been holding the slip of paper open it and read what you had written *before* the construction of the magic square. Your spectator would read: "I predict that the magic total will be 93!" You will, seemingly, have predicted the total.

Let us first illustrate this principle using a nine-celled square. Let us assume that your spectator calls the number 27, and that you decide to construct a nine-celled square using this number. To determine the "prediction" or subsequently arrived at magic total you must perform the following computation: Multiply spectator's number by 3, and add 12 to the product. In this case, 3 times 27 is 81, and 81 plus 12 is 93. You would thus "predict" 93. After handing the prediction to one of the spectators, construct a nine-cell square beginning with number 27. Your finished square should be as below. Point out that a magic total

34	27	32
29	31	33
30	35	28

of 93 has been arrived at, and show how the lines, rows, diagonals etc. all add to this magic total. Have your prediction opened and this will add a nice finish to your efforts.

Using a 16-cell square requires a different computation. For a 16-cell square you do the following: Multiply spectator's number by 4, and add 30 to the product. To show how this develops, let us assume that your spectator calls the number 31. You secretly multiply this by 4 (4 times 31 is 124) and add 30 to the product (124 plus 30 is 154). In this case, you would predict 154 as the magic total. Construct a 16-cell magic square, starting with 31. The finished square is shown below. Note that all of the relationships inherent in the other 16-celled square apply to this square.

46	32	33	43
35	41	40	38
39	37	36	42
34	44	45	31

For a 25-cell square you must do the following: Multiply by 5 and add 60. As an example, let us assume that your spectator calls the number 12. You secretly multiply this by 5 (12 times 5 is 60) and add 60 to the product (60 plus 60 is 120). You would thus predict 120 as the magic total. Develop the five by five square, starting with 12, and the finished square will appear as follows:

28	35	12	19	26
34	16	18	25	27
15	17	24	31	33
21	23	30	32	14
22	29	36	13	20

(5) set squares

Up to this point I have discussed the production of magic squares which are constructed by following easily understood patterns of construction. These squares seem to flow into formation when you follow the simple necessary rules or steps. There is a tremendous field involving squares which have what I call set patterns. Basically, these squares have predetermined cell positions for which there does not appear to be any pattern of construction. Thus, if you wish to use these squares you must simply memorize the position of each cell.

Of course, with the constant use of any set squares you will develop great facility with them. Your memory can be abetted by jotting down the set squares you wish to use on small cards which can be conveniently carried. Before demonstrating one of these set squares simply look for an opportunity to glance at the square you plan to use so that your memory can be refreshed.

Here are examples of two set squares, and an entertaining stunt you can perform with each.

A. The Birth-date Square. This is a demonstration using a spectator's birth-date in combination with a nine-cell square. Using the various numbers which make up the spectator's birth-date, you fill in a nine-cell square with a resultant magic total. However, all during the course of this demonstration your spectator has apparent control of the different values you insert in each cell!

To demonstrate this stunt you must memorize the order of the positions as shown in the following square. Restated, the first number you will insert is placed in the position indicated by 1, the second number is inserted in the position indicated by 2, etc.

8	1	7
5	6	3
2	9	4

To demonstrate, draw a nine-cell blank square and request that someone call out his birth-date. Let us assume that someone calls out March 17, 1898. You convert this to number values and write 3–17–98 above the blank square (3 represents the month of March, 17 is the 17th day, and 98 of course represents the year 1898).

(a) Insert 98 in position 1.

(b) You will now work with either the 3 or the 17. Give your spectators a choice. Let us assume that 17 is chosen. You now ask your spectators if they wish to have you add this to 98 or subtract it from 98. Let us assume that they elect to have 17 subtracted. Subtract 17 from 98, and enter 81 (the remainder) in position 2. (Note: If the date mentioned is in the 20th century you may have to eliminate the choice of subtraction as this could lead to a negative number, which would not work successfully. You can easily determine this by performing the simple subtraction before offering your spectators the choice.)

(c) Continue by again subtracting 17, but this time it is taken from 81 (the last number entered). The result is 64, and this is placed in position 3. You point out that the numbers 98, 81, and 64 are "important numbers" and will be used in your next steps.

(d) The square, at this point, will appear as follows:

3 — 17 — 98

	98	
		64
81		

You now work with the number 3. Once again offer your spectators a choice of either adding or subtracting with the number. Let us assume that they choose to have you continue to subtract. You subtract 3 from 98 (one of the "important numbers") and insert the result, 95, in position 4 in your square.

(e) 3 is now subtracted from 95 and the result, 92, is placed in position 5.

(f) You now use the next "important number," 81. Subtract 3 from 81 and place the result, 78, in position 6.

(g) Subtract 3 from 78 and place the result, 75, in position 7.

(h) You now use the last "important number," 64. Subtract 3 from 64 and place the result, 61, in position 8.

(i) Your last step is to subtract 3 from 61 and place the result, 58, in position 9. Your finished square will appear as follows:

3 — 17 — 98

61	98	75
92	78	64
81	58	95

Of course, it is clear to your spectators, all during the above steps, that you are using the numbers *they* designate and that you are adding or subtracting, as per *their* instructions. When the square is completed, show that it has magical possibilities because even though your spectators controlled the numbers and/or the addition or subtraction . . . it totals 234 by line, row, or diagonally. Hand the finished square to the spectator whose birth-date was used, and tell him that not only is 234 a lucky number for him but that carrying the magic square with him will also result in his carrying his own good luck. (Note: If you construct the magic square on the reverse side of your business card your spectator will also have a reminder of you and your business organization.)

By following the above procedures, the magic square will always be produced. Either the 3 or the 17 can be used first, and the number worked with can either be added or subtracted (as long as subtraction will not bring you into negative numbers). But once you start to add with a number (as per your spectator's instructions) you must carry through and add with it. If you start to subtract, you must then complete all of the steps continuing to subtract. As the dates used are varied, or as the procedure using the same date is varied, a different magic total will result, but a perfect nine-cell square will always result.

Once you have properly memorized the necessary set square, the placing of the various values follows a pattern and will flow into a smooth presentation.

As another example of this square, let us use the birth-date April 7, 1927. Convert this into 4–7–27. 27 is placed in position 1. Let us assume your spectators choose the 4 as the first number for you to work with, and also they want you to add with this number. Add 4 to 27 (31) and place 31 in position 2. Again add 4, but this time to 31 (35), and place 35 in position 3. Mention that 27, 31, and 35 are the "important numbers" which will be used in your next steps.

You now work with the 7. Give your spectators the choice of having you add or subtract with the 7. Let us assume that they choose to have you subtract. Subtract 7 from 27, the first "important number," and insert the remainder, 20, in position 4. Subtract 7 from 20 and insert the remainder, 13, in position 5. You now work with the next "important number," 31. Subtract 7 from 31, and place the remainder, 24, in position 6. Subtract 7 from 24 and place the remainder, 17, in position 7.

You now work with the last "important number," 35. Subtract 7 from 35 and place the remainder, 28, in position 8. Subtract 7 from 28 and place the remainder, 21, in the ninth and last position.

The finished square is illustrated below, and it bears the magic total 72.

4 — 7 — 27

28	27	17
13	24	35
31	21	20

B. Controlling a Total. This stunt is performed with a 16-cell square. You have your spectators select a number which later proves to be the magic total.

The choice of the number is suggested at between 34 and 60. 34 is the lowest possible total in a 16-cell square, barring negative or fractional numbers, and although you can offer a range greater than 60, the larger total will require larger "key" numbers which may stand out and appear obvious.

Again, a set square is utilized. The square is constructed as shown on the next page.

The 13th, 14th, 15th, and 16th positions are your "key" positions which will control the square to attain the total selected by your spectator. These positions must be memorized.

30 / 14	1	12	7
11	8	29 / 13	2
5	10	3	32 / 16
4	31 / 15	6	9

In demonstration, you begin to fill in the square as shown above. After inserting about half of the numbers (of this memorized square) ask a spectator to name a number between 34 and 60. Let us assume that he chooses the number 50. After learning this number continue to fill in the square up to the 13th position.

At this point you must make a simple calculation: You must subtract 21 from the number your spectator has named. In this case, you would subtract 21 from 50 for a remainder of 29. You would then insert 29 in the 13th position, 30 in the 14th position, 31 in the 15th spot, and 32 in the 16th position. The finished square will appear as the above square. Note that you now have a four by four magic square rendering the magic total 50 vertically, horizontally, diagonally, by corner squares, the four corners, etc.

As an additional example, let us assume that the number 42 was selected. You would fill in up to the 13th position. At this point you subtract 21 from 42, for a result of 21. Insert 21, 22, 23, and 24 in the 13th, 14th, 15th, and 16th positions respectively. You now have the following square totaling 42 in the various combinations:

A painless method of performing this is to have your square all filled

22	1	12	7
11	8	21	2
5	10	3	24
4	23	6	9

out, up to the 13th position. This should be on the back of a business card or small sheet of paper. You must memorize the 13th through 16th positions, or write these in very lightly. Don't show this prepared square to your spectators. Instead, talk about magic squares and state that you would like to demonstrate one that is quite fascinating. Apparently make the square, actually faking the action. (Use care so that your spectators don't realize that you are working with a prepared square.) After a few moments, request that a number between 34 and 60 be named. Perform your single calculation, make your entries in the correct positions and, with a minimum of memory work, you will have completed the square.

(6) their move

This unusual magic square was performed by an English mathematician, Mr. F. Parnell, over thirty years ago. It is a five by five (25-cells) square which permits your spectator to place whatever number he wishes in whatever cell he chooses. From this starting point, you complete filling in the cells to result in a perfect magic square.

This system follows the general procedure as in the regular 25-celled square, but with two important variations.

(a) Instead of moving each consecutive number in an oblique direction (one-to-the-right and one-above), each move is made one cell to the right and *two* cells up.

(b) When the last number written is divisible by 5, then the next number is placed two cells to the right of it.

As in the regular odd-celled squares, the top and bottom lines are considered as continuations of each other, and the left and right rows are also considered as continuations.

For convenience in describing this square, we will confine the numerical selection from 1 to 25. Let us assume that your spectator decides to start with 11, and he puts it in the circled position shown below. By following the two up and one to the right rule, you fill in the square as the one below. Note that rule "b" is followed in that each number divisible by 5 has its following number placed two cells to the right of it.

14	2	20	8	21
10	23	(11)	4	17
1	19	7	25	13
22	15	3	16	9
18	6	24	12	5

Note that after inscribing 25, the next number written is 1. And you continue up to 10, at which point the square will be completed.

In the following diagram you will note a square developed with 14 being the first number, and the starting position is second from the left on the bottom line.

17	10	23	11	4
13	1	19	7	25
9	22	15	3	16
5	18	6	24	12
21	(14)	2	20	8

This is one of literally thousands of magic squares which each have their unique variations. It is impossible to memorize the endless varieties, but it is amusing to be able to do a few of the more interesting ones.

(7) costello's tic tac toe

A Tic Tac Toe contest (or game) is actually played on a surface exactly that as used in a nine-cell magic square. Realizing this, Martin Gardner mentioned, to mathematics instructor-engineer Don Costello, the possibility of working this into an unusual combination of effects. Costello worked on Gardner's original idea and developed it into a workable form. In time, with the addition of suggestions from several mathematicians and magicians, the original Costello effort has been refined into a practical and surprising stunt.

Basically, a game of Tic Tac Toe is played between the performer and a spectator. Instead of using a pencil and pad, playing cards are used as markers for each participant's move. The performer indicates his moves by placing his cards face down in the positions he chooses, and the spectator places his cards face up. Of course, the object is for one of the contestants to place three of his cards in a line, row, or diagonal. This, as in most carefully played Tic Tac Toe contests, results in a tie . . . no winner. However, upon turning all of the cards face upwards it is seen that a perfect magic square with the magic total 15 has emerged from the contest! Your spectator freely makes his moves, yet the result is always perfect.

It is not necessary to actually draw a Tic Tac Toe board when demonstrating this as the positions can easily be visualized.

It is necessary to prearrange the nine cards used in the following order of values: ace (1), 8, 2, 7, 3, 4, 5, 6, 9. A simple way to remember this is to place the cards in consecutive order running from ace through 9, then simply shift the 8 and 7 to the positions indicated above. Also, it is suggested that all of the cards used be of the same suit.

Let us assume that you have the nine cards of the Heart suit arranged in the above order. Place the packet on the bottom of the deck of cards, and place the deck in its card case. The 9 of Hearts should be at the bottom of the deck and the ace of Hearts should be nine cards above it.

To perform, discuss Tic Tac Toe and volunteer to show how the game can be played by using playing cards as markers instead of the conventional methods. Permit a spectator to give the deck two complete riffle shuffles. (This will not disturb the order of the nine set-up cards, it will merely distribute them throughout the deck.)

After the shuffle, take the deck and run through the cards, holding the cards face upwards, and remove all of the Heart spot cards from ace to 9 inclusive. As each card is removed place it face down on top of the previously removed cards. To all appearances you will have removed nine Heart cards in a random order, but they will actually be in your prearranged order.

Either draw a Tic Tac Toe surface or suggest an imaginary board. Fan the packet of nine cards between your hands, faces toward you, and divide the packet in two parts so that your left hand holds the top six cards and your right hand the bottom three.

State that you will make the first move, and do so by placing the top face down card of those in your right hand (5 of Hearts) in what should be the center position of the Tic Tac Toe board. After your initial move your hands should still be separated, holding their various cards face downwards.

Ask your spectator to point to the position he wishes to select as his first move. He can either point to a corner square (one of the squares located on the four corners of the board) or a side square (one of the four positions located between the corner squares).

If he points to a corner square place the two cards (held in your right hand) on *top* of those held in your left hand and place the packet of eight cards face down on the table.

If he points to a side square place the two cards on the *bottom* of those held in your left hand and place the entire packet face down on the table.

Let us assume that a corner square has been selected. Your spectator is instructed to remove the top card from the packet of eight cards (after you have placed the cards on the table, as above) and place this face upwards in the position he has chosen. Let us assume that he places his card in the square as in fig. 1. (Note that *all* corner squares are in the same relative position from the center square. Thus, by revolving the playing area, any corner square chosen is exactly the same as any other corner.)

Your second play must be on *either side* of the corner *diagonally opposite* your spectator's corner. Thus, your second play is either X or Y as shown also in fig. 1. Assuming that each player makes moves to keep the other from winning, from this point on all moves are self-forcing. Of course, all of your moves are made by placing your cards face downwards, and your spectator places his markers (cards) face upwards. The game should result in a tie, and after all nine cards are distributed in their respective positions, turn all of the cards over so that they are face upwards and show the magic square which has evolved during the course of play. In this instance, the square in fig. 2 will result.

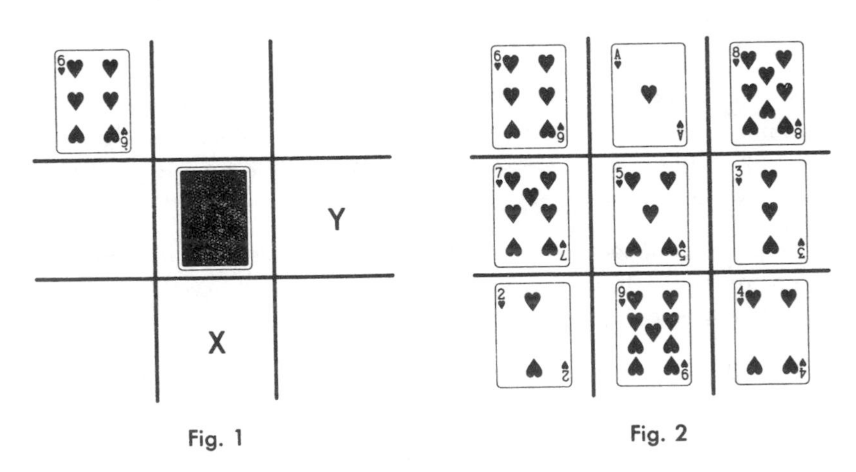

Fig. 1 Fig. 2

Should your spectator's first play be to a side square, the strategy employed is different than that used above. Let us assume that your spectator selects the side square as indicated in fig. 3 as his first move. (Of course, as soon as your spectator indicates a side square you would place the cards held in your right hand to the *bottom* of the group held in your left hand.) Your spectator would then take the top card of the packet, and place it face up in position, fig. 3.

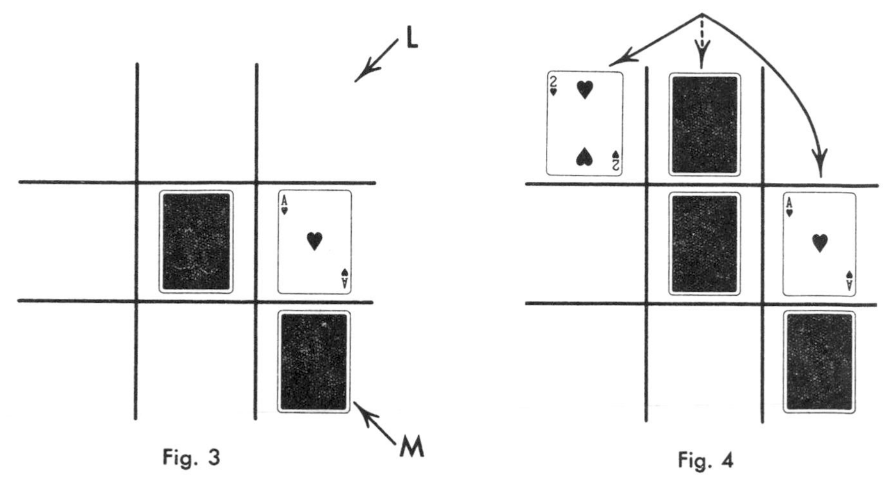

Fig. 3 Fig. 4

(Note that, again, if the Tic Tac Toe area was revolved every side square would be in the same relative position to the center square.)

(a) Your second move (after your spectator's initial side square move) is made to a corner on either side of your spectator's position. This could be either L or M in the above diagram. Let us assume that you choose position M.

(b) Your opponent, to keep you from winning, is now forced to play in the corner diagonally opposite your last move, indicated by the two of Hearts (fig. 4).

(c) Your next move is to the side square that contacts both of your opponent's previous plays. This is indicated by the arrows in the above diagram.

(d) Your spectator's next move is forced in that he must play (in this example) in the center square of the bottom line to keep you from winning.

(e) Your next play is to the corner adjacent to your spectator's last play (fig. 5).

(f) The next plays, on to the finish of the game, are self-forcing.

If you follow the above correctly, the finished magic square, after the tie game, will appear as the one shown below (fig. 6). There are two possible magic square finishes . . . that shown here, and a mirror image of this square.

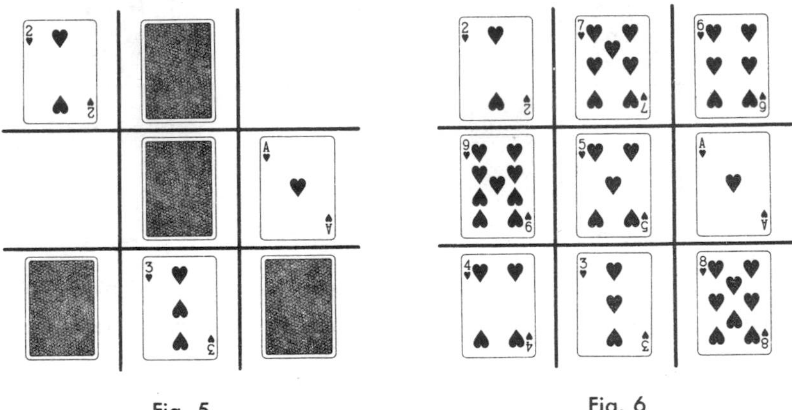

Fig. 5 Fig. 6

After a few trials you will fully understand the procedures. This is an amusing demonstration and a surprising departure from typical magic squares.

Chapter 6

magic with ordinary objects

One of the great assets of knowing something about mathematical magic is that so many intriguing stunts can be performed with ordinary objects which are readily available. In this chapter I have included a selection of just such material.

Business cards are always available, and so are coins. Matches are invariably at hand, and so are paper and pencil. I've included unusual applications with these, and other, common objects.

Occasionally, certain minor preparations are necessary to be able to perform certain effects. Don't allow this minimum of necessary effort to deter you from learning and performing the effect in question. Prearranged or prepared material, if unsuspected by your viewers, can be doubly effective because you not only have this "going for you," but you have the underlying mathematical principle as well.

The first item, Dinner Ware, is a perfect after-dinner trick that you can perform at any time.

(1) dinner ware

You have just completed dinner and you are still at the table. You borrow several objects, or simply use some of the things which are still on the table: a knife, an ash-try, napkin, etc. One of the spectators is asked to think of one of the designated objects. "I want you to think of any one of these things," you say. "Just concentrate on the name of the object of your choice. Would you mind standing and turning away from the table? (Spectator stands and turns away from the table.) I am going to tap various objects with my pencil. Everytime you hear me make a tap I want you to silently spell one letter in the name of the object you are thinking of. When I have tapped enough times so that you have completed spelling the name of the object you are to indicate this by calling: Stop!"

The spectator, who is turned away from the table, listens for your taps and silently spells one letter for each of your taps. When he calls "stop" he is asked to name the object he has thought of and to turn towards the table. Upon turning around the spectator sees that your pencil is on the object he thought of! Your last tap was on the mentally chosen object!

This is presented in the form of a mental trick, but I've included it in this chapter because although it is effective it does not have the full flavor of a mental experiment. In most of the mental stunts you are able to actually name or predict something specific. In this effect you actually produce no information, but the results would have it appear that you do.

The principle relies upon a selection of objects which each spell with a different number of letters. Let us assume that the following objects are available for this stunt: a bun, knife, fork, napkin, ash-tray, and cigarette.

Observe that each of the objects spells with a different number of letters, and they are listed in ascending order:

bun 3 letters
fork 4 letters
knife 5 letters

napkin 6 letters
ash-tray 7 letters
cigarette 9 letters

Other objects, and additional items, can be used. You must contrive to avoid duplication of items which spell with the same amount of letters.

Let us assume that you are working with a group of objects as listed above. Place the objects on the table, clearly naming each item (so that a mental picture of the spelling is conveyed to your spectators). Request that a spectator think of one of the objects, and that he turn away from the table while you tap the various objects. Let us assume that he is thinking of the knife.

You start by random tapping the first two times (tapping any objects). At this point, your spectator will have spelled: k-n, the first two letters of the object he is thinking of.

Your 3rd tap *must* be on the object which spells with three letters, the bun. (Your spectator will have spelled: k-n-i.)

Your 4th tap is on the object which spells with four letters, the fork. (Your spectator will have spelled k-n-i-f.)

Your 5th tap must be on the object which spells with five letters, the knife. (At this point your spectator completes spelling the word (k-n-i-f-e) and he calls "stop.")

Have the spectator name the thought of object and turn to face the table. He will be surprised to see that your pencil is on the mentally chosen object. The other spectators present will vouch for the fact that you didn't move the pencil after being told to stop, and that you mystically have managed to land at the right spot at the right time. (Of course, your spectator need not turn around during the tapping process, but I find this little touch adds to the overall effect.)

You actually tap in the proper numerical progression of the objects. It doesn't matter which object is thought of as your pencil will always be on the correct object when your spectator completes his spelling. In this example, there weren't any objects used that spelled with 1 or 2 letters. So the first two taps were made on any objects. In addition, no object was used with 8 letters. In actual practice, your 8th tap could be on any object, and your 9th tap on the cigarette (a 9-letter speller). As an alternative, let us assume that "stop" was not called by the time you completed your 7th tap. This would automatically inform you that your spectator thought of the cigarette. Instead of continuing the tapping procedure you could conclude by saying: "It isn't necessary for you to spell any more as I have a distinct impression of what you are thinking of." Dramatically name the cigarette, and you have an excellent alternative ending.

(2) avis' variation

A clever English magician, Jack Avis, worked out a variation on this general theme which may be of interest to you. This is a fine example of how a principle may be employed using a different premise and approach to completely change the appearance and results of the basic effect.

This effect uses a deck of playing cards as a convenient means of showing an unusual coincidence. You can adapt this to books, magazines, or some other medium.

You remove a deck of playing cards, in its case, and hand it to a spectator so that, "I can't tamper with the cards in anyway." You also remove 4 cards, each bearing a series of unrelated numbers, as shown below. The cards are introduced as "Spanish Bingo" cards and each of four spectators are handed one of the cards.

1	2	3	4
81 31 59 26	72 29 67 68	23 27 28	41 42 52
44 55 49 32	76 71 89 24	38 75 33	51 62 66
65 45 82 54	85 84 39 25	37 79 83	61 46 56
21 36 64 22	35 47 43	74 87 88	
69 86	34 53 57		
	58 63 48		

"These cards are from a new game called Spanish Bingo. You will notice that the numbers are not in proper sequence, and that they sort of ramble all over the cards. Well, in Spanish Bingo the object is not only to have the correct numbers covered, as in regular bingo, but speed is an important factor. The player who declares bingo first is the winner."

You propose to use these Spanish Bingo cards in an interesting experiment. Each of the spectators who is holding a card is asked to think of one of the numbers listed on his particular card. A mental selection is made by each of the four spectators, and after they have set their minds on their numbers the Bingo cards are collected by the performer.

The deck of cards is removed from its case and the performer spreads them face upwards to show that the cards are not in any particular order. The deck is squared and turned face down.

The performer says: "You are now each thinking of a number. I am holding a deck of 52 cards in my hands, and you were given a choice of numbers from 1 to 88. Instead of counting to each of the numbers you have selected we are going to spell to each of your numbers. We will do so one at a time, and for each letter in the number you are thinking of I will remove one card from the deck. For example, let us say one of you thought of the number 2. I remove the first card and you mentally spell: T. The next card and you spell: W. The next card and you spell: O. At this point, having completed your spelling, you would say: stop." As the last few sentences are spoken, the performer removes 3 cards from the top of the deck to illustrate the manner in which each spectator is to perform his spelling.

The first spectator, let us call him spectator A, is asked to think of the number he has selected, and as the performer deals one card at a time from the top of the deck (onto the 3 already dealt in the above illustration) he spells a letter in the number he has selected. When spectator A completes his spelling he calls stop. The card which is on top of the deck at the completion of A's spelling is removed from the deck and handed to A to hold. Its face is not revealed.

This exact procedure is continued with spectators B, C, and D until each has spelled the number he thought of, and each has a card.

At this point the performer talks about the sympathy that exists between Spanish Bingo players, and how it is obvious (to the performer) that the four spectators have a latent ability for the game of Spanish Bingo. The proof of this is shown when the spectators are told to reveal their cards, and it is discovered that each holds an ace. The four aces have been discovered in this random manner!

To perform this stunt you must make up the 4 cards as illustrated above. I suggest that you type them neatly, and carry them between plastic or celluloid pieces and they will last indefinitely.

You will note that the 4 Bingo cards appear to be without any relationship. However, all of the numbers listed on card 1 spell with nine letters, card 2 spells with ten letters, card 3 spells with eleven letters, and card 4 spells with eight letters.

Before performing, place the aces in the following positions from the top of the deck: 13th, 24th, 36th, and 45th.

To perform, remove the card case and have someone hold it. Remove the Spanish Bingo cards explaining what these unlikely objects are as suggested above. Be sure to hand card 1 to spectator A, card 2 to spectator B, 3 to C, and 4 to D. Always hand the cards out clockwise so that you will have no difficulty in remembering who has which card. Your spectators must spell in proper A, B, C, D sequence or else the order will not correspond to the positions of the prearranged aces.

After each has selected a number, gather the Bingo cards together and put them away. (Note: You can have a duplicate set of Bingo cards, but with a true random placing of the numbers. At the conclusion of the stunt you can bring out this duplicate set, and your spectators will be at a complete loss to understand the workings of the trick. A subterfuge, but a most effective one!)

To continue, remove the deck from its case and spread the cards, without changing their order. The deck will appear to be ordinary and without preparation.

Illustrate the manner in which each spectator is to spell his number by spelling T-W-O (as you remove the three top cards). After this example, have spectator A mentally spell his number. When he calls stop you should have dealt off the last card onto the discard pile. Hand the top card of the deck (an ace) to him and request that he not look at it and that he keep its face from the view of the other spectators.

Continue, as above, in B, C, D order. Build to your climax, and the end result should be quite startling. If you have prepared a duplicate set of Spanish Bingo cards, casually remove them so that the suspicious can be further deceived.

This is a novel adaptation of controlled spelling wherein there appears to be a free choice and wide selection. There are several magic tricks, with entirely different effects and end results, which are now on the market. They utilize the same principle, but are quite unique in conception. Since these are commercial items I am not able to discuss them at this time. But with some imagination you can develop your own approaches and effects with this limitless principle.

(3) personality test

This is a variation of an idea Bob Hummer originated and included in his pamphlet, "Three Pets."

Your spectators will see you remove, or borrow, a quantity of business cards. Handing the cards to a spectator, you request that he place the cards behind his back. While the cards are behind his back (or under a table if you are all seated) he is to reverse the two top cards of the packet and give the packet a simple cut. He is to continue to reverse two cards at a time, and cut the packet, until he is satisfied that there can be no control or knowledge by anyone regarding the condition of the cards: how many cards will be blank side up or printed side up. As you can see, the combinations are many. (Specific combinations are actually 40,320. But this would be *specific* positions for each card. This is based upon $1 \times 2 \times 3 \times 4 \times 5 \times 6 \times 7 \times 8$.)

"I have analyzed your personality," the performer says to the spectator, "and I am positive that you are a 5–3 person. No question about it. You can cut the cards and continue the reversing process as many times as you wish, but I feel positive that you are a 5–3 personality."

After the spectator is satisfied with his reversing and cutting of the packet, he brings the cards forward. You slowly spread them out and it is discovered that 5 are facing in one direction and 3 in the other. The performer has correctly analyzed the spectator as being a 5–3 personality!

The cards are ordinary, and upon your spectators attempting the same effect they will not be able to predict or control the results—unless they do so by pure chance.

Only 8 cards are used, and they may be your own or borrowed. One side of each should be blank, and the other side with printed matter.

Show that the 8 cards are all facing the same way, blank side upwards or printed side up. Don't over-emphasize this, but be certain that the condition of the cards is noted. When you hand the packet to your spectator you must secretly reverse the bottom card of the packet of 8. To do this without problems, ask your spectator to turn around. When he turns around it will be a simple matter to turn over the bottom card of the packet (you should be holding the packet between both your hands). Do this noiselessly. Have him extend his hands behind his back, and hand the packet to him. Ask him to face you, but to keep the packet behind his back as he carries out the reversing and cutting process. In this innocent way you will have properly set the packet for the climax.

If seated at a table your task is equally simple. Just hand the packet to your spectator under the table, and reverse the bottom card as soon as the packet is out of sight and just before they reach your spectator's hands.

Your spectator now goes through the process of reversing the top two cards and gives the packet a simple cut. This is carried on as many times as the spectator wishes.

As your spectator performs the reversing and cutting operations you begin to discuss the fact that you analyze him as a 5–3 personality. When your spectator finally brings the packet forward spread the cards out slowly and dramatically. 5 of the cards will be faced one way (either blank side or printed side up) and 3 faced the opposite to the above. This will confirm your 5–3 analysis.

Upon examination you will note that after your secret reversal of one card and your spectator's initial reversal of two cards, each subsequent move of his retains the 5–3 relationship established . . . or nearly so. For example, after your spectator's first move let us say that 3 cards are blank side up and 5 printed side up. From this point, your spectator can only make three possible moves:

1. He turns two of the printed cards over, which results in 5 being printed side up and 3 blank side up. (This still retains a 5–3 relationship.)
2. He turns one printed and one blank over. This still retains a 5–3 relationship.
3. He turns 2 blank cards, which results in a 7–1 relationship.

The 3rd contingency is very remote, and if it does occur, the spectator's next reversal of 2 cards returns the packet to the 5–3 relationship. However, it is just possible that your spectator may end in a 7–1 relationship. Should this occur (and it is very rare) you simply repeat the experiment, stating that you feel that your analysis can't be that poor and that you would like to have your spectator try it again.

Thus, your spectator, during the course of his moves, will either retain a 5–3 relationship or, if a 7–1 situation evolves during the course of his moves, his next move will return the packet to the 5–3 relationship.

Should your spectator attempt to duplicate the effect, when you hand him the packet of 8 cards be certain that they are ALL facing the same way. Starting in this condition, there can be no control over the final result.

(4) a matchical experiment

This is an interesting stunt that was shown to me, in a slightly different form, many years ago. I haven't been able to determine the originator.

Wooden or paper matches are used, as they may be carried around comfortably. However, other counting units may be used if matches aren't available (paper clips, coins, sugar-cubes, etc.).

Let us assume that you plan to use a box of small wooden matches, the size used for lighting cigarettes. The box should be filled to capacity, with at least 40 or 50 matches.

To perform, you remove the box of matches and hand them to a spectator. From this point, you turn away from the proceedings as you give your spectators the following instructions:

(1) Request that the matches be removed from the box and that your spectators make 3 piles of matches, each pile to contain the same number of matches and the amount decided upon is to be a free choice. Of course, the amount in each pile is kept secret. Thus, each pile could contain from 1 match to 15 or 20 matches.

(2) The piles should be in a line, running from left to right, so that you may refer to them as piles A, B, and C; with pile B being the center pile.

(3) Let us assume that your spectator has secretly placed 7 matches in each pile. The situation will be as follows:

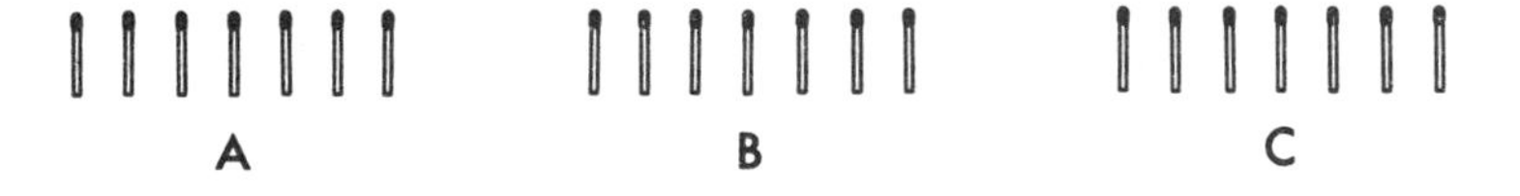

(4) You now instruct your spectator to remove 3 matches from piles A and C, and have these added to those in pile B. If your spectator has done this correctly, the situation will now be as follows:

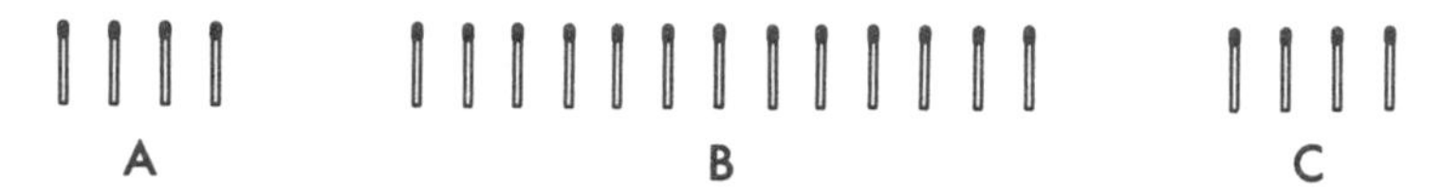

(5) You now have all of the matches remaining in pile A placed aside with the surplus matches, those not used in this experiment. Only piles B and C will remain.

(6) Your next instruction is for your spectator to count the number of matches now in pile C. He is to remove from pile B an amount of matches equal to that of pile C. In this case, your spectator will count 4 matches still in pile C, and he will therefore remove 4 matches from pile B.

(7) Your spectator is next instructed to take pile C, plus the matches just removed from pile B, and place these with the discards. There will only remain pile B after the above has been carried out.

(8) "It was impossible for me to know how many matches you started with, or how many were in each pile. I could have no idea as to how many matches are left, is that correct?" you ask. (At this point there will actually be 9 matches remaining in pile B.)

(9) You now request that you be handed as few or as many matches as they wish from pile B. Thus, you may be handed none, 1, 2, or even all of the matches, if they so elect. Upon receiving these matches (with your back still towards your spectators) you bring your hand to your forehead, touching your head with the hand containing the matches. Let us assume that you were handed 4 matchees. You positively state that: "I have a distinct impression of 5 matches remaining on the table." And you will be absolutely correct!

The method is well concealed during the various operations. To determine how many matches are in pile B *before* you are handed any matches you do this by multiplying the number of matches you asked them to move (in step 4) by 3. In this case, since you asked your spectators to move 3 matches from each of the end piles to pile B, you would multiply 3 × 3 for a result of 9. Thus, at step 9 you know that 9 matches are on the table *before* any were handed to you. Upon being handed 4 matches, you merely subtract 4 from 9, and correctly announce the remainder: 5.

You always multiply, by 3, the number of matches you instruct your spectators to move from piles A and C and add to B. If, for example, you had instructed them to move 2 matches from each of the end piles to the center pile, there would be 6 matches in pile B (3 × 2) prior to performing step 9.

The mechanics of this are quite simple. When they remove from B the same number of matches remaining in C (step 6), they will leave pile B with three times the number originally added to B. To give you an obvious example, let us assume that only two piles are used, A and B. Let us also assume that 7 matches are placed in each pile at the start. Your first request is that 3 matches be moved from A to B. (This leaves A with 4 and B with 10.) Your next instruction is to remove from B a number equal to those remaining in A. As 4 matches remain in A, 4 matches would be removed from B, leaving 6 matches in B. These 6 matches are *two* times the number originally added to B. (As you only worked with two piles you would multiply the number moved by 2.) The operation should now be apparent. The use of three piles instead of two is what helps conceal the obvious.

Note that four, five, and in fact, an infinite number of piles may be used. You merely increase the value of the number you multiply by 1 for each pile added. Three piles, however, are quite sufficient to throw off the keen observer, and the effect moves quicker with this minimum number of piles. (You would never perform this with only two piles as the workings would be quite obvious to your spectators. Two piles are just used for illustrative purposes to give you a clear picture of the method.)

(5) out of time

Stewart James is one of the very original mathematical-magical creators presently active. He often combines this talent with a dash of whimsy. This idea of Stewart's combines an original twist with a surprise ending . . . which will result in a good laugh.

In effect, you remove your wrist-watch and adjust the hands on the dial "To read or indicate a number I am predicting." Of course, you don't permit your spectators to see the setting you make so as not to spoil the climax of the effect. The watch is placed on the table with the face of the watch downwards.

A deck of cards is removed and a spectator is invited to deal out 10 piles of cards. 4 of the top cards of the piles are selected, in a completely fair manner, and used as value units in the experiment. You say, "I have predicted a number by using the numerals of my watch. You have selected 4 cards in a fair manner. I want you to add together the value of the cards. For example, if they were a 2, 3, 1 (ace), and 9 they would total 15. Remember this total. I now want you to multiply the 4 cards by themselves. For example, you would multiply $2 \times 3 \times 1 \times 9$ for a total of 54. You now subtract 15, the first total, from 54, the second total, to arrive at a random figure . . . the number I have attempted to predict."

Upon following your instructions your spectators find that the sum of the 4 cards totals 8, and the multiplication of the value of the 4 cards also totals 8. Therefore, the result of subtracting one total from the other results in zero! You appear to be in an embarrassing dilemma. However, a spectator is asked to turn over your watch, and it is discovered that you have predicted correctly: *the hands on the watch are missing,* indicating that you've predicted nothing!

Your first requirement is a watch from which you remove the hands. This should be an old watch, no longer serviceable, or you can purchase an inexpensive wrist-watch and remove the hands from the face of the watch. (This is guaranteed to confuse the hapless jeweler selling you the watch.) Place the watch on your wrist prior to performance, and don't give it a thought. There is very little likelihood of anyone noticing this unusual condition.

You must prearrange the following 10 values on the bottom of a deck of cards prior to performance. Set the following cards on the bottom: 2, 4, ace, ace, 2, 4, ace, ace, 2, and 4. They may be in any suit order, but the numerical sequence must be maintained. (After the cards are arranged, place the deck in its case and leave it there until you are ready to perform this stunt.)

To perform, state that you are going to make a prediction, but to add a touch of novelty you will use your wrist-watch as a medium through which to predict a number. Remove your watch without permitting anyone to see the dial, and go through the motions of setting the hands at specific numbers. Go to great pains to be precise, even though this is all subterfuge.

Place the watch on the table with the dial downwards, and remove the deck of cards to proceed with the effect. Remove the deck from its case and remove all of the picture cards (kings, queens, and jacks) commenting that you only wish to use cards with a direct numerical value since you have made a prediction, gesturing towards your watch.

Hand the remaining 40 cards to a spectator, and ask him to deal out 10 piles of cards, face downwards, one card at a time. (At the conclusion of this deal-out your prearranged set of 10 cards will each be on top of one of the piles.)

Hand a pencil to a spectator and ask him to place the pencil across the tops of any 4 piles he desires. He is to remove the top cards from each of the piles so selected. (In this way, your spectator is restricted to any consecutive run of 4 of your prearranged cards.)

Upon removing the 4 cards he is to:

1. Add them together, using their numerical values. (They will total 8.)
2. Multiply the cards by themselves. (The product of this multiplication will be 8. Example, $1 \times 1 \times 2 \times 4$ equals 8.)
3. Subtract one total from the other. (8 from 8 leaves zero!)

Upon learning that the result is zero, the performer appears somewhat disturbed. Finally, the prediction is inspected, and your spectators will acknowledge that you are correct as the absence of hands on the watch dial indicates that you have predicted nothing!

As you will no doubt observe, the selection of cards is restricted solely to combinations of the following values: 1, 1, 2, and 4. Added or multiplied, the result will always be 8. An off-beat emanation from Mr. James!

(6) one to eight

George Sands, a clever creator and full-time performer of magic, developed this interesting number trick using 4 squares of paper.

Tear a sheet of paper into 4 fairly equal squares. On the top square write 1, and on its reverse side write 2. On the next square write 3, and on its reverse side 4. On the next square write 5, and on its reverse side 6. 7 and 8 are written on their respective sides of the last square. The following diagram shows you how the 4 squares will appear.

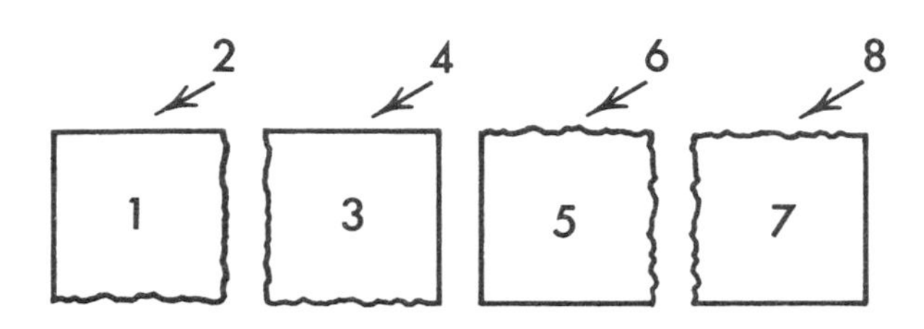

There are many unusual stunts you can perform with these squares, and I will confine this explanation to two of the applications:

1. *There are two methods for performing a prediction.*
2. *You can perform a mind-reading stunt.*

Let us first deal with one of the prediction methods. You write a prediction on a card and hand it to one of your spectators for revealment at the conclusion of the experiment. One of the spectators is handed the 4 squares of paper and he is instructed to place them on the table so that only odd values show. He is now requested to turn over any one of the odd values he desires. (Let us assume that the odd values (1–3–5–7) are upwards, and your spectator turns the 7 over. You now ask that the values of all the numbers showing be added together. (1–3–5–8.) The total reached is 17. Your prediction is inspected, and it will be found that you have predicted 17!

Once you are aware of the relationship of the numbers, the explanation is elementary. When performing this item you *always* predict 17. The 4 odd values always total 16. However, when any one is reversed it will add a value of 1 to this total (the even numbers always being 1 higher than the odd numbers on their reverse sides). Thus, by following the procedure as outlined above, the total arrived at will always be 17. This progression of plus 1 is constant regardless of which odd slip is reversed.

The second prediction effect is similar to the above, but in this effect your spectators are instructed to leave any 2 of the odd numbers turned upwards, and any 2 of the even numbers. To perform, you *always* predict 18 when performing this variation. The sum of any combination of two odds and 2 evens always is 18. To explain, the total of 1 plus 2 plus 3 plus 4 plus 5 plus 6 plus 7 plus 8 is 36; one-half of 36 is 18; thus, by leaving any 2 odd and any 2 even face upwards you are equally cancelling out one-half of the sum of all 8 sides. This leaves a remainder of one-half of the total value: 18.

The mind-reading experiment is performed as follows: After turning away from a spectator, he is requested to pick up the 4 squares and mix them. He is next asked to place them on the table with any of the numbers upwards that he wishes. He is next asked to concentrate upon the total of the numbers he has chosen to leave turned upwards. (Let us assume that the following surfaces show: 2, 8, 3, and 6.)

You appear to be having some difficulty in "receiving the impression of the total." You say, "The odd numbers always seem to confuse me. Please concentrate on the odd numbers. How many odd numbers are showing?" In this example you will be told that one odd number is showing. You appear to brighten up and say, "I'm getting it clearer now. I've got it. Let's see . . . the total is 19!"

The method is as follows: 16 is your key. To 16 you must add 4, minus the odd numbers showing. In this example only one odd number was showing, so you add 3 (4 minus 1) to 16 for a total of 19.

If 2 odd numbers were showing you would add 2 (4 minus 2) to 16 for a total of 18. If 3 odd numbers were showing you would add 1 to 16 for a total of 17 (4, less the 3 odds showing). If 4 odds are showing you add nothing to 16. If no odds are showing you add 4 to 16.

You will note that the relationships, apparent in the two prediction experiments, are evident in the last item. It is possible to develop variations on this theme, and carry Sand's basic ideas much further, but you will find that for impromptu performance, and ease of action, the above uses will stand up very well.

(7) time and money

Another example of the fine thinking of Jack Yates is evident in this novel approach. 12 pennies are arranged to form a clock face. In the diagram to follow, note that a packet of matches is placed at the top of the dial to indicate 12 o'clock so that there will be no confusion as the effect progresses.

The performer now turns his back from the table, and continues the effect through to its conclusion without seeing the table or the movements of the coins.

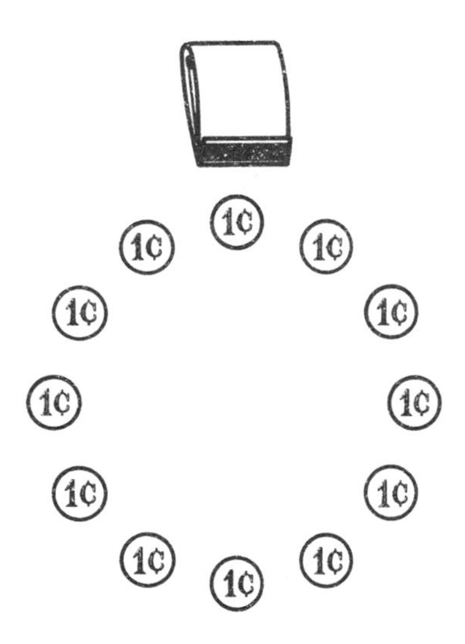

(1) A spectator is invited to turn over *any* six of the coins, so that six heads and six tails will now show. The performer is not told which coins have been reversed.

(2) The performer now requests that the coins at the following hour positions be reversed: 1, 4, 5, 8, 9, and 10. (If a coin at any of the positions is heads up it would be turned tails up; if tails up it would be turned heads upward.)

(3) You now ask how many heads are showing, without being told which positions are occupied by the heads upward coins. There are seven possibilities: 0, 2, 4, 6, 8, 10, or 12. Suppose you are told that there are four heads up. Announce that you will divide the 12 coins into two equal heaps so that there will be 2 heads and 4 tails in each heap. Without knowing the positions of the heads or tails, this appears to be impossible.

(4) You do this by having your spectator remove the following coins from the dial: a) The two coins that indicate ten minutes past twelve, b) The two that indicate five minutes to six, and c) The two that indicate a quarter past seven.

It will be found that you have removed two heads and four tails, leaving the identical order still as part of the clock dial. You have successfully divided the coins into equal groups.

Before going into the explanation I would like to point out that it may happen that after your spectator has reversed six coins, and after the six you name are reversed, it is possible that all twelve coins will be heads up or tails up. If this happens, stop right there. As Yates declares: "Any reasonable man will agree that, though your back was turned, you must have known exactly what coins had been reversed. And that, by our standards, is a miracle!"

To proceed to the preponderant instances when the above "miracle" will not occur, the effect is actually self-working. The coins *you* had reversed (1, 4, 5, 8, 9, and 10th position) are *not included* in those you had removed. You actually have the coins at the following positions removed in step 4: 2, 3, 6, 7, 11, and 12. However, calling them as specific times ("a quarter past seven," etc.) helps conceal this fact. Thus, you are removing the complement of the reversed coins. The division will thus be equal.

You may develop other combinations if you wish. The above is not difficult to remember, and it is quite clear in translation to your spectators.

Chapter 7

magic with playing cards

Of all branches of mathematical magic, that which is concerned with playing cards is perhaps the most prolific and exciting. The structure of cards leads to this ever-widening road of discovery. Cards, for example, may be used as single counting units. The faces and backs are also a point of distinction. The red suits and black suits may also be utilized in various ways.

The face of each card bears a numerical value (permitting the jacks, queens, and kings to represent 11, 12, and 13 respectively), and an additional point of separation is that the cards may be divided into even face values and odd face values.

As you can see, the various combinations of the above characteristics, applied to 52 distinct playing cards, can lead to virtually endless possibilities. This is borne out in that in the world of magic and magicians new card effects, methods, and techniques are the most common developments. This does not necessarily depreciate the quality of the card items developed, but points up the fact that a new coin trick, for example, is exceedingly rare, whereas new card tricks and ideas appear with delightful regularity.

The application of mathematics adds a new dimension to card magic. A few years ago a magazine was devoted exclusively to card effects solely dependent upon mathematical prearrangements of the cards. Several booklets and pamphlets have been devoted exclusively to mathematical card tricks. And there are many card "classics" which are well known among magicians as well as the public. These are passed from individual to individual, each explaining the mathematical principle essential to the trick, so that these hoary yet still wonderful tricks (to the uninitiated) will probably be performed many generations from now.

There have been remarkable developments in mathematical card magic during the past two decades, and I would like to comment on just one of these facets before discussing several mathematical card tricks which I believe will break fresh ground for all but the most up-to-date conjuror.

Quite recently the Perfect Faro Shuffle has come into prominence among the more advanced card-workers. A Perfect Faro Shuffle requires that the deck be cut into two exactly even halves, and that each section of 26 cards be so interlaced that they perfectly alternate with each other. Thus, after the performance of one Perfect Faro Shuffle the top card will be the card originally occupying the top position, the card second from the top will be that which originally occupied the 27th position, the card third from the top would have originally been in the 2nd position, the card fourth from the top would have originally been in the 28th position, and so on throughout the deck. The following diagram shows the inter-weave of the top 8 cards before the two halves are pushed together.

Ed Marlo, a brilliant card worker and creator of card magic, has written two excellent booklets on the Faro Shuffle. *The Faro Shuffle,* by

Marlo, discusses various techniques for performing these perfect shuffles. Marlo's *Faro Notes* describes many exquisite card stunts that depend upon the use of Perfect Faro Shuffles. Of course, basically these are mathematical applications of an efficient manner of controlling cards to specific positions.

An oddity of the Perfect Faro Shuffle is that 8 perfect shuffles will return a full deck of 52 cards to its original starting arrangement. (Note: The original top and the original bottom cards never change their respective positions during the 8 perfect shuffles.) Another interesting sidelight is the movements of the 18th and 35th cards. These two cards alternate positions with each shuffle.

Of course, I don't expect the casual reader to develop the ability to perform Perfect Faro Shuffles, but I did want to mention a new technique—based on mathematics—which is gaining great favor among the more sophisticated card magicians.

To perform card stunts with a high-interest quotient it is necessary to veer away from cumbersome (and sometimes never-ending) counting tricks. Endless piles stacked upon endless piles of cards, with a punchless ending, can be quite discouraging. Thus, the following material will have good visual appeal and, for the most part, require a minimum of repetitive actions.

The first item, The Mathemagician, is a trick that was first published in a book I wrote on card tricks several years ago. I've simplified the handling so that it requires no skill. This effect does require a minimum of dealing, but the startling climax is well worth it.

(1) the mathemagician

In simplified form, the effect is that of two spectators dealing a random number of cards to eventually form 4 packets. When the top card of each packet is revealed it is seen to be an ace . . . the 4 aces have been discovered in a random fashion!

Before performing, remove the 4 aces and place 2 on top of the deck and the other 2, together, at the center of the deck. Return the deck to its case and you are ready for performance.

To perform, remove the deck of cards from its case as you ask two spectators to come forward to assist you. Hold the deck face upwards between your hands and run the cards between your hands, from left to right, to show that the cards are free of obvious arrangement. When you arrive at the 2 aces which are together in the center of the deck, separate the deck at this point so that the 2 aces join the cards you have thumbed into your right hand. You should now be holding one-half of the deck in each hand, and each half will be face upwards with 2 aces at the bottom of each half.

Place the two packets on the table, faced upwards, and square the packets. Your situation should appear as follows:

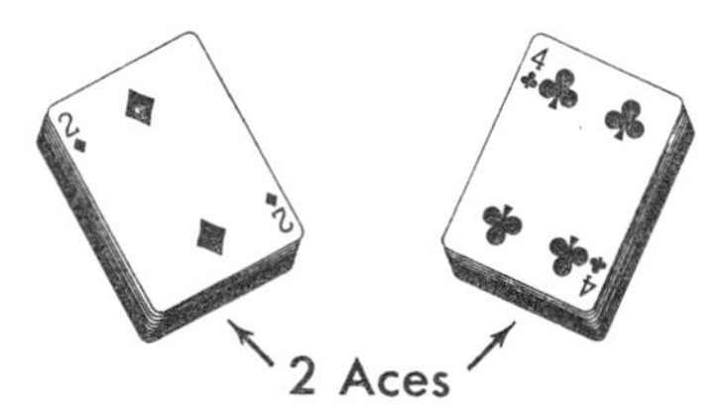

Place a packet in front of each spectator and discuss the reactions of individuals to various conditions. You could say, "People react differently to similar conditions. But if a sympathy exists between them they will always tend to develop similar results. I am going to show you how, even though each of my two assistants will react differently, they will retain a certain evidence of sympathy."

Place your right thumb at the base of one of the packets and slowly riffle the cards by running your thumb upwards, towards the top of the packet:

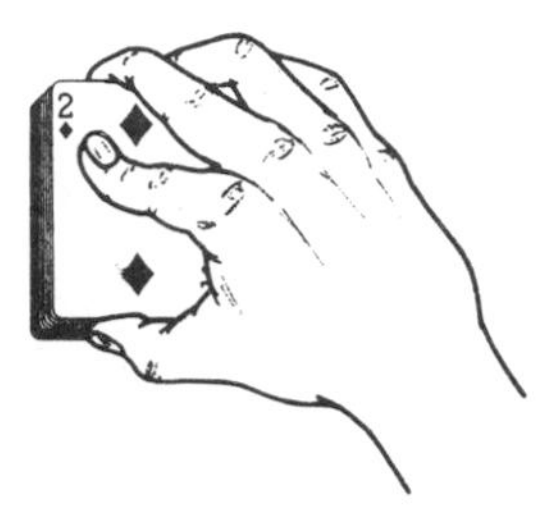

To the spectator closest to this packet say, "I want you to call stop whenever you wish, and when you react by saying stop, I will stop riffling at that point."

When spectator calls stop you cease riffling the cards and lift off all of the cards which have not yet been riffled:

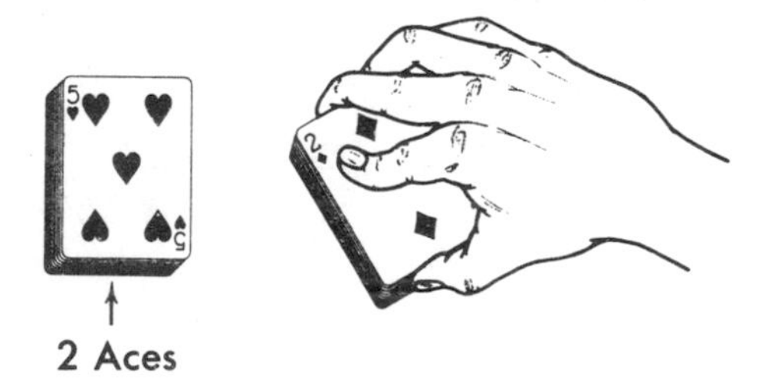

Discard the packet lifted off. If your spectator does not call stop by the time you have completed riffling the entire packet simply start over again.

Repeat the same sequence, as above, with the second spectator and the second packet. At the conclusion of this phase you will have 2 face up packets remaining on the table (2 aces at the bottom of each) and they should be of unequal thickness. Point out that each spectator stopped you at a different position, each reacting in his individual manner.

Turn each packet face down (being careful not to expose the aces at the bottom of each packet), and hand a packet to each spectator. Each spectator is now to deal cards from his packet singly, one on top of the other, and each is to stop dealing whenever he wishes. At the conclusion of this phase each spectator will have dealt a packet of cards on the table, and each will still have some undealt cards. Take the undealt cards from each spectator and discard them. Again, point out that each spectator has reacted differently in that one dealt more than the other, one stopped sooner than the other, one dealt faster than the other, etc.

Instruct each spectator to square up the pile of cards he has dealt, and each is to pick up his dealt pile. The first spectator is now instructed to deal out his cards singly, into two piles, by alternately dealing from one pile to the other until his cards have been exhausted. Next, the second spectator is to perform the exact same actions as did the first. At the conclusion of this phase each spectator will have 2 piles in front of him.

Be sure to point up the variations in the amount of cards each has, whether or not each ended with an odd or even number of cards, and whatever differences you can note between the actions of each spectator.

"Even though each spectator has acted independently, and though there could have been no control over the deals, I am going to prove to you that a sympathy exists between these two people." As you say this, slowly turn over the top card of each of the 4 packets, and the 4 aces will appear!

This is a most surprising conclusion to the effect. The deal-outs take very little time and are usually of great interest as your audience will be curious to see how each spectator reacts to your various instructions.

Of course, it doesn't matter how many or few cards the spectators individually decide upon. If the above instructions are carefully followed, the 4 aces must gravitate to the top of each of the final packets. Magicians will look for a mathematical explanation to your method, and mathematicians will seek "a magician's means," thus, you will be able to puzzle both.

(2) relatively speaking

As I have mentioned several times, a principle that is well known can be quite puzzling . . . if properly cloaked. Using a method quite well known, an arrangement of cards in consecutive numerical sequence, I have used it in this effect in a manner that has baffled several extremely clever mathematician-magicians.

In effect, the performer removes a card for himself, for example the Ace of Spades, and inserts it (behind his back) face upwards into half of the deck. The performer permits the spectator to note that his card is the Ace of Spades.

The spectator is now given the remaining half of the deck and he is told to remove whatever card he chooses to select. He is to remember this card, but he is not to show it to the performer. The spectator is asked to place his card in the center of the performer's packet for about half its length, so that the situation at this point will appear as follows:

The performer says: "By pushing your card into my packet it would result in adding a card to my packet. Instead of adding a card, let us allow your card to displace one of mine. Therefore, please remove the card either directly above or directly beneath your protruding card." The spectator removes the card which is either above or below the projecting card and puts this "displaced" card on the table. The projecting card, spectator's selection, is now pushed squarely into performer's packet.

"There is an interesting relationship that now exists. I placed the Ace of Spades face upwards into my packet. I did this behind my back so that you would have no idea as to what position I placed it. You inserted your card face down into my packet at a freely chosen position. In doing so, you displaced a card. We are going to use the displaced card in an interesting way. We are going to use its value to see if there is any relationship between my card, the Ace of Spades, and your card."

The "displaced" card is turned face upwards, and its value is noted. Let us assume that it is the 5 of Clubs. Point out that the value 5 will be used.

The performer spreads his packet between his hands, from left to right, until he arrives at the face up Ace of Spades. He places the Ace of Spades and all of the cards above it, onto the table. He now slowly counts to the fifth card and removes the card occupying that position. The spectator is asked to name the card he selected, and upon turning the card face up it is seen to be the spectator's card! The spectator placed his card in perfect relationship to the performer's card!

Confine this effect to cards that have a white border. Arrange the following on top of the deck, prior to performance: 10 cards running from ace (1) to 10 in numerical sequence. Any suit order may be used, but the top card should be the ace, next the 2, and so on through to the tenth card (the 10). The Ace of Spades should be in the center of the deck. Place the arranged cards on top of the deck, place the deck in its case, and you are ready to perform.

(1) Remove the deck from its case, turn the deck face upwards as you remove an "obvious card." When you reach the Ace of Spades place it face up on the table and state that you will use this card for yourself. Square up the deck, turn it face downwards, and hand it to a spectator.

(2) Ask the spectator to cut off about half of the cards and hand them to you. (Your 10 prearranged cards will be on top of the packet handed to you as this will be the original top section of the deck.) Hold the packet face down in your left hand, and hold the Ace of Spades face up in your right hand. State that you are going to place the Ace "Somewhere in my packet, but I will do this behind my back so that you can't see to what position I place it." Place your hands behind your back to apparently carry out this action. Actually, place the Ace face up on top of the face down packet held in your left hand and cut about 6 cards from the *bottom* of the packet onto the *top* of the packet. Bring the packet forward and place it face down on the table. By using cards with white borders it will be impossible for your spectators to know the position now occupied by the Ace of Spades.

(3) Request that your spectator shuffle the half of the deck he has been holding, and that he withdraw any card he desires. He is to remove the card and remember it. He is now requested to place his card face down "Into the center of" the performer's packet, but he is to leave it projecting, as before. (If you are in doubt as to whether or not your spectator has placed his card into your prearrangement you can remove his card, hand it to him, and say, "You've got the idea. Now try and put your card right into the center of my packet." This will cover you for situations wherein your spectator will place his card too near the top or bottom of the packet.)

(4) Discuss the "displacement" idea, and have the spectator remove either the card above or below his (protruding) card. After he has removed a card, have the spectator push his selection squarely into your packet.

(5) For the climax, pick up the packet and run the face down cards into your right hand. When you arrive at the face up Ace of Spades remove it plus all of the cards which were above it, and place them on the table. Have the "displaced card" turned over, and count to its value with the cards remaining in your left hand. At the exact final count will be the spectator's card.

This elementary arrangement of values, running from 1 to 10, may appear as an obvious solution, but performed as outlined above I can assure you that it will deceive well-informed subjects. The "displaced card" simply reveals its position (from the face up Ace of Spades). The spectator's card has simply replaced it. The freedom of having the spectator remove the card either "above or below the projecting card" will add to the puzzle, but not increase your work!

(3) two hummer gems

The very original Mr. Bob Hummer has developed more effects using the faces and backs of cards than any other magical creator. The following two items are examples of Hummer's brilliant approach. They are most conveniently performed while seated at a table, but you can easily apply these tricks to other conditions.

A. The Match-up. The performer removes a group of cards from a deck and openly shuffles half of them face up into the other face down half. The cards are now handed to a spectator, and he is requested to place the melange of face up and face down cards beneath the table and give them a thorough overhand shuffle so that there can be no doubt that the cards are hopelessly mixed. When the spectator is satisfied, he is asked to remove the top 10 cards and place them on the table. The remainder is handed, under the table, to the performer. After a moment, the performer brings his packet forward and places it on the table.

The performer asks: "Do you believe that I could exactly match the number of face up cards in your packet with those in my packet?" After the spectator's reply the spectator is asked to spread out his packet and count the face up cards which are there. Let us assume that 6 cards are face up. The performer's packet is now slowly spread out to reveal that it, too, has exactly 6 cards face up!

The effect may be immediately repeated.

This pleasant stunt requires no preparation, no skill, and it is quite direct. Remove 20 cards from a deck, turn 10 face upwards and shuffle them together with the other 10 cards. The result will be a mix of face up and face down cards. Hand the packet to a spectator and ask that he place the packet underneath the table. He is to shuffle the cards while they are under the table (using an overhand shuffle) until he is well satisfied that the cards are completely mixed.

The spectator is now asked to count off the top 10 cards and place them on the center of the table. The remaining cards are handed to the performer under the table. When the performer receives the packet he performs no complicated action. Under the table he simply reverses the entire packet handed to him so that the original top will now be the bottom, and the bottom will now be the top. When he has performed this simple revolving action the packet is brought forward and placed on the table.

The spectator is now asked to spread his packet and note the number of face up cards in it. Let us assume that the spectator finds he has 6 face up cards in his packet. Upon spreading the performer's packet it will be noted that he, too, has 6 face up cards!

To repeat the effect, the performer picks up his packet and places it on top of the spectator's packet. However, as the performer's packet joins the spectator's packet the performer simply revolves his packet (this will result in the combined 20 cards consisting of 10 face up and 10 face down cards). The 20 cards are now handed to the spectator, and the exact sequence is followed as above.

For a clear understanding of the mechanics of the effect, shuffle 10 face up cards into 10 face down cards. After thoroughly shuffling, remove the top 10 cards and spread them out. Let us assume that 3 are face up and 7 are face down. The remaining packet must thus consist of 7 face up and 3 face down. However, by turning the remaining packet over (reversing it) you will have changed the complementary condition to an exact match up!

During the course of the effect you never actually know how many cards will be face up in the spectator's packet. You may give the impression that you do know this if you wish, as a presentation of this sort will materially add to the effect.

B. Reversed Location. In this effect, which handling I've slightly altered from Hummer's original, a packet of cards is handed to the performer beneath the table. (If performed while standing, the cards may be placed behind the performer's back.) The performer shuffles them and then hands them, still under the table, to a spectator. With the cards hidden from view the spectator is asked to give the packet a simple cut. He is now instructed to turn over the top 2 cards. Another simple cut is now performed. Again, the spectator turns over the top 2 cards, and then cuts them to the center of the packet. This procedure of reversing the top 2 cards and cutting them into the packet is continued until the spectator agrees that the cards are in a completely disorganized condition.

All of this has been carried out with the cards hidden from the view of everyone present. When the spectator is satisfied with the reversing and cutting, reversing and cutting, he is asked to bring the packet into his view. He is to look at the card now on top of the packet. "Is the card face up?" the performer asks. If the card is face upwards the spectator is told to remember it, turn it face down, and cut it to the center with a simple cut. Further, he is now permitted to give the packet additional simple cuts, under the table.

If, when the spectator looks at the top of the packet, the card there is face down the spectator is instructed to turn it face upwards, remember it, and cut it (now face up) into the center of the packet with a simple cut. Additional simple cuts may now be performed under the table.

The packet is now handed to the performer under the table. The performer "mixes" the cards, still hidden from view. The performer then says, "You turned an unknown number of cards face upwards and cut them into the packet. The packet is in a completely disorganized condition, and from the packet you have selected a card which was arrived at purely by chance. I am going to attempt a startling feat. Watch!" The packet is placed at the center of the table, the spectator names his card, and the packet is immediately spread out. ALL of the cards are faced the same way with the exception of one card. The one reversed card is the spectator's selected card!

To perform, have a deck shuffled and less than half the cards handed to you. Place the packet beneath the table, and under the guise of "mixing them thoroughly" you perform the following actions: You must secretly reverse every alternate card so that the cards in all the odd positions (1, 3, 5, 7, etc.) will remain face down while the cards in all the even positions (2, 4, 6, etc.) will be face up. To do this, push the top card of the packet to the right and take it in your right hand. Push the next card to the right, but use the card in your right hand to lever it over so that it will fall face up on top of the cards in your left hand. Now take this face up card under the card held in your right hand. The next card is taken off face down and under the two held in your right hand. Use the cards in your right hand as a lever to turn the next card (fourth card) face up onto the packet. Take this card under those in your right hand. The next card is taken face down under those held in your right hand. You continue this procedure until you have exhausted the cards. However, you must end with the last card being taken as a face up card (the packet must have an even number of cards). If the packet handed to you was originally an even number of cards you will have no problem as the last card will be a face up card. However, if the last card is a face down card simply allow it to slip from your left hand onto the floor. No one will notice this (as you will be performing these actions with the cards beneath the table) and you can recover the card at a later time.

Hand this arranged packet, under the table, into the waiting hands of one of your spectators. Tell him to cut the packet a few times. He is now to turn the top 2 cards face up on top of the packet, and then give the packet a simple cut, losing the 2 reversed cards somewhere in the packet. He is to continue this process of reversing the top 2 cards and cutting them until he feels that the cards are in complete disarray.

When he is satisfied, request that he bring the packet into view so that only he can see the top card of the packet. If it is face up he is to remember it, turn it face down, and give the packet a simple cut. (If it is face down he is to turn it face up, remember it, and give the packet a simple cut.) In either event, the packet may now be given several simple cuts. The packet is now returned to the performer beneath the table.

Upon receiving the packet the performer apparently shuffles the cards. Actually, the exact action of alternately reversing all of the even positioned cards is repeated: The top card is taken in the right hand, next card is turned over and taken under the card in right hand, next card is taken under those in right hand, next card reversed, etc. When you have completely run through the packet it is brought forward and placed at the center of the table.

It doesn't matter if the packet appears face up or face down. Tap the packet with your hand, have spectator name his card, and spread the packet out. The selected card will be the only reversed card in the packet! A surprising climax.

The method is ingenious in operation. With alternate cards reversed, a condition you developed when first handed the packet, the spectator's actions of reversing the 2 top cards and cutting the packet ad infinitum will not in anyway destroy the constant alternation. Your spectator and the other viewers will be convinced that the cards are becoming hopelessly mixed face up and face down, but the orderly alternation will remain.

When your spectator brings the packet forward and "only into his view" and reverses the card he is to remember, he is actually throwing only that one card out of perfect alternation. When you are handed the packet for the second time, you will bring all of the cards back into their original order except for the one card the spectator threw out of sequence . . . the selected card. And so this will be the one card which will be reversed (faced opposite) in the spread packet.

(4) the spirit mathematician

This is a fascinating revelation, dependent upon the various permutations of totals possible with a minimum of numbers. It first appeared in 1920, in a booklet of original card effects by the clever creator,

Mr. Charles C. Jordan. Many years later, it still retains two commendable virtues: 1.) It is still a most effective demonstration, and 2.) Its mathematical principle is well concealed.

Basically, your spectators would see you take a well shuffled deck of cards and place it in your jacket pocket. Anyone would next be requested to name any card of his choosing. Let us assume that the card named is the Four of Clubs. You would then reach into your pocket and remove a card. "I have removed a card that will indicate the suit you have named." Upon turning the card over it is noted that it is a Club.

"I will now try to find a four spot, to duplicate the card you have named. I think I've got it!" and a second card is removed from your pocket. It is shown to be a four. You have thus removed a card to indicate the suit and another the value of the freely named card!

The method is described in the opening sentence of this trick . . . but with a few extra subtleties. By using 4 values by themselves or in various combinations, it is possible to produce any number from 1 to 13 (ace to king). The 4 values used are 1 (ace), 2, 4, and 8. Obviously, if a card having a value of 1, 2, 4, or 8 was required you would simply use the value corresponding. However, let us assume that a value of 3 was required. This is produced simply by using the 1 and the 2. If 5 was required, the 4 and 1 would be used in combination. 7, for example, would involve the 1, 2, and 4.

As you can see, by using the 1, 2, 4, and 8 either alone or in various combinations you can reproduce any value from 1 through 15, although you need only run up to 13 when performing this stunt.

Prior to performance, remove the following cards from your deck and place them in the given order in your jacket pocket: Ace of Clubs, Two of Hearts, Four of Spades, and Eight of Diamonds. The remainder of the deck is placed in the card case. (You must remember the suit order. You can reproduce any of the 52 cards with these four cards.)

It is suggested that you precede this stunt with a card trick or tricks which will not require any of the above cards so that, when you do perform this effect, your spectators will believe that you have been working with a complete deck of 52 playing cards. To perform, have the deck thoroughly shuffled and openly place it into your jacket pocket (in which you have previously set the 4 cards). Place the deck alongside the 4 cards so that they are easily accessible.

A spectator is asked to name any card he wishes. Let us assume that he names the Seven of Hearts. Place your hand in your pocket and appear to be running your fingers through the cards. Actually, since the cards are in 1, 2, 4, 8 order, and since you know the proper suit sequence, you will have no problem in removing the proper cards. First remove the card indicating the suit. In this case you must remove the Two of Hearts. Remove it from your pocket, giving the impression that it has come from the center of the deck. Turn it face upwards, first commenting that the first card will indicate the suit of the named card. Show the Two of Hearts, proving that you have been successful.

State that you will remove additional cards to add to the value of the Two until you reach the value of 7. Place your hand in your pocket, and after suitable by-play, bring out the 4. "Four and Two total 6, so I will have to find an Ace to reach the exact value you named," you state. Put your hand back into your pocket and dramatically remove the last card (the Ace) and reveal that you have been able to find cards to correctly indicate the freely named card.

With a minimum of thought you will quickly note how simple it will be for you to adjust to the various combinations. Always bring out the card equal to the named suit before you go after the value cards. You can then use this card as a part of the total, if necessary, or ignore it and bring out whatever other card or cards are necessary to build towards the value of the named card.

If, by chance, a spectator should name one of the 4 set cards, you then have pretty near a miracle on your hands. Just enter your pocket, appear to be "feeling" for the exact card, and bring it out. It will be very difficult to top this!

(5) the college bet

I remember this as "the college bet" because it was shown to me by a man who claimed that he made enough money betting on this proposition to send his son through college. This was an obvious exaggeration, but it is an interesting percentage gambit.

The proposition takes the following form: You state that anyone may shuffle a deck of cards as thoroughly as he wishes. The deck is then cut into three face down packets. You now state: "I am willing to bet even money ($1 to $1) that an ace, a jack, or a four will be on top of one of the piles."

It appears that you have the short end of the proposition. In the next few paragraphs you will learn why it is actually to *your* advantage to offer just such a bet.

An even money, or fifty-fifty, bet is one in which you have an equal chance to win as you do to lose. For example, in tossing a coin the chances are fifty-fifty that you will correctly name the side that will fall upwards. It may fall either heads up or tails, thus, you have one way of winning out of two possibilities.

With a deck of cards, an even money proposition would be one in which you would have 26 ways to win out of 52 (since there are 52 cards in a deck). Stating that an ace, jack, or four will be found on the top of one of the three piles appears to confront you with many ways to lose and only a few ways to win.

However, you actually have a better than fifty-fifty chance. Thus, if you have made an even money bet you have a definite advantage.

This is how your advantage is produced. Before any card is turned over there are obviously three possible ways of winning: with the card on top of the first, second, or third pile, respectively. The probability of winning with the first card is 12 (the number of aces, jacks, and fours) out of 52 (the total number of cards in the deck) or 3/13.

The probability of winning with the second card is equal to 40/52 (the probability of an indifferent card on the first pile) *times* 12/51 (the probability of a winning card on the second pile), or 40/221.

The probability of winning with the third card is equal to 40/52 (the probability of an indifferent card on the first pile) *times* 39/51 (the probability of an indifferent card on the second pile) *times* 12/50 (the probability of a winning card on the third pile), or 12/85.

The total of these three probabilities (3/13, 40/221, 12/85) is the probability of your winning the bet by turning up an ace, jack, or four in three tries. It turns out to be 47/85, or a little better than 55%.

There are actually 22,100 3-card combinations in a deck of 52 cards $\left(\frac{52 \times 51 \times 50}{3 \times 2 \times 1} = 22{,}100\right)$. Combinations *excluding* Aces, Jacks, or Fours total 9,880 $\left(\frac{40 \times 39 \times 38}{3 \times 2 \times 1} = 9{,}880\right)$. Subtracting the "misses" (9,880 combinations) from the total possibilities (22,100) results in 12,220 wins or "hits." Thus, there are 2,340 more ways to "hit" than "miss" out of 22,100 total combinations.

(6) counter cards

Basically, this is an unusual use of what would normally be quite an obvious application of simple mathematics. But masked in the veneer of a card mystery, it can have a more profound impact.

Your spectators are requested to shuffle a deck of cards. After the shuffle, you are handed the deck and you have one of the spectators choose a card. The card is replaced in the deck, the deck is squared up and placed face down on a table. One of the spectators is asked to lift off about ¾ths of the deck, leaving a small packet on the table. The small packet is turned over (face upwards) and whatever value shows is counted to from the remainder of the deck. For example, let us assume that the Six of Diamonds is on the face of the small packet when it is turned over. You ask that the spectator who retains the main portion of the deck count six cards off this section and into a small pile.

The pile just dealt is turned over (face upwards). Let us assume that the Four of Spades shows on the face of it. Your spectator thus deals another small pile, but this time consisting of four cards, alongside of the other piles.

The pile just dealt is now turned face upwards. Let us assume that the Three of Clubs shows at the face of this pile, as diagram below shows. Your spectator deals three cards into another pile, and when this last pile is turned over the selected card is discovered at the face of it.

The above effect can lend itself to amusing presentation by having the performer go through apparently involved computations during the various deals. The final discovery of the selected card should be surprising and will defy all known laws of mathematics!

Your work is quite simple. After the deck is shuffled it is necessary for you to learn the value of the top and bottom cards of the deck. To do this, simply take the shuffled deck and hold it face upwards as you comment, "You really shuffled the cards very well and you are making this difficult for me. But pure mathematics will always survive adversity." Let us assume that the bottom card is the Six of Diamonds and the top card is the Four of Spades. Just remember the values 4 and 6. As soon as you have the necessary information turn the deck face downwards and proceed with the trick.

Spread the deck between your hands for the selection of a card, but as you do so, mentally add together the values of the top and bottom cards. In this case, the combined value is 10, and so you must remember 10 as your key. As you spread the cards between your hands, mark off the card which is tenth from the top (you secretly count the cards as you spread them). When a card is chosen, take all of the cards from the marked off position into your right hand, leaving the original bottom portion of the deck in your left hand, and exactly 10 cards in your right hand. Your spectators will believe that they have withdrawn a card and that you have simply divided the deck into two sections.

After your spectator has noted his card, extend the cards held by your left hand towards your spectator so that he may place his card on top of this packet. After he does this, place the cards held by your right hand on top of those held in your left hand and neatly square the deck. It will appear that you have fairly had the chosen card replaced, but you have actually contrived to bring it eleventh from the top of the deck . . . below the top 10 cards.

Place the deck on the center of the table and point out that one of your spectators will now carry out all of the physical work while you will do all of the "difficult" mathematical work.

(1) Ask one of the spectators to lift off about ¾ths of the deck.

(2) Have the small packet turned face upwards and have the value of its face card noted. In this case, the Six of Diamonds will show.

(3) Have six cards dealt into a small packet. Have this packet turned face upwards and the value of the face card noted (the Four of Spades will show in this example).

(4) Have four cards dealt into another small packet. This last dealt packet is now turned face upwards. Let us assume that the Three of Clubs shows on this last packet. At this point, things should appear as on p. 175 with a portion of the deck still being held by one of the spectators.

(5) Have three cards dealt from the portion of the deck still being held, and when this last packet is turned face upwards you will find the spectator's selected card at the face of it.

Before discussing the mechanics of the trick, it should be obvious to you that you always add together the top and bottom cards of the deck and use this total as your key. If a 7 and a 9 were on the top and bottom your key would be 16 and you would have to have your spectator replace his card beneath the top 16 cards of the deck. Performed casually, you will have no difficulties. Remember, your spectators have no idea as to what you are doing, and all of the necessary actions are very simple and open.

To describe the working of the trick, the first packet turned up is the original bottom of the deck. You form the second pile (in this case, six cards) by dealing from the top of the deck. After the first deal the original selection is fifth from the top of the deck.

When you turn over the second packet, the original top card (a four) will be noted. The third pile, consisting of four cards, is now dealt. This results in bringing the originally chosen card to the top of the deck, and an indifferent card is now at the bottom of the third pile. When the third pile is turned over (the four card pile) the indifferent card shows; and when you deal the fourth pile, the chosen card is the first card dealt, and will therefore be the face card when this pile is turned face upwards.

A few trial runs and you will thoroughly understand not only how the trick operates but how to perform it. It will be of great interest to mathematicians as they will be seeking an involved percentage solution while you are actually using an extremely simple, but well concealed method.

(6) the four queens

This is an effect that I developed a few years ago, and one which I have expanded into many variations. I will describe what, to my mind, is the most direct approach and is perhaps the most puzzling. Before reading the method see if you can work it out. Run through the description with cards in your hands as you read so that you will get a clear understanding of the various instructions.

In effect, a deck of cards is shuffled and one half is retained by the performer, the other half being given to a spectator. Each places his cards behind his back and removes 4 cards from his packet: The performer removes 4 cards and places them in a pile on the table, face downwards; and the spectator also removes 4 cards as did the performer. The remainder of the deck is placed aside.

The spectator is invited to mix each of the packets. The performer says: "We have each withdrawn 4 cards from different parts of the deck, and you have mixed each of the packets. You must agree that neither of us can have any knowledge as to the cards or the positions of any of the cards in each of the packets. I am going to give you complete control over the movements of the cards during this experiment. But first I am going to turn my back, and when I do so I want you to place one of the packets on top of the other so that we will be dealing with a combined packet of 8 cards. You may place my packet on top of yours, or yours onto mine, whatever you wish."

The performer turns away from the table and the spectator assembles the two packets in whichever order he prefers. The spectator is instructed to hold the packet of 8 cards in dealing position, and the performer now faces the spectator and continues to face the action during the remainder of the effect.

(1) The spectator is told that he may do one of two things: a) He may deal the top card face down on the table and then place the next card to the bottom of the packet he is holding; or b) He may place the top card to the bottom of the packet and deal the next (2nd) card down on the table. The spectator takes his choice.

(2) He is next instructed to repeat step 1, as above, so that he will have dealt two cards down on the table (in a small pile of two cards) and also placed two cards to the bottom of the packet . . . in whatever sequence he chooses.

(3) To the right of the packet of two cards he is again to perform steps 1 and 2. At the conclusion of this phase, there will be two packets of cards on the table, and each packet will consist of two cards. As you can see, up to this point the spectator has been given the opportunity to deal (or place to the bottom) each of the cards handled, and so there are many combinations of results possible. This should be pointed out.

(4) The spectator returns to packet A as diagrammed below. He is again allowed the sequence of moves as in step 1. There will now be 3 cards in packet A and only 2 cards in packet B.

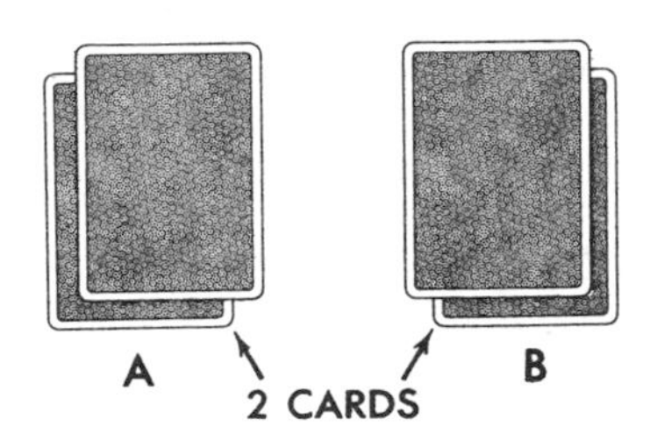

(5) The spectator repeats step 4, but does so over packet B so that there will now be 3 cards in each of the packets.

(6) The last 2 cards the spectator holds are dealt one each on the packets so that each now consists of 4 cards.

The performer points out that the original cards are now so co-mingled that it is virtually impossible to know where cards of each original packet are now located, what specific cards where chosen, and the order or condition of the packets. The spectator is asked to place his hand on one of the piles. The other packet is discarded. The spectator turns over the packet selected and it is found to consist of the four queens. Almost a mathematically impossible coincidence!

Do you have the solution? Be assured that deception, as well as mathematics, is essential for the success of this trick.

For the perfectionist the following preparation is necessary: Remove the four queens (or whatever four cards of the same value you decide to use) and place them in one of your back pockets. If you can't prepare as above, simply set the four queens on top of the deck prior to performance. Place the deck in its case and you are ready to perform.

If you have secretly set the queens in your back pocket you may then offer the deck out for shuffling before performing this trick. You may also precede it with any card experiments which do not rely upon your having a full deck of 52 cards. When ready to perform, have the spectator take half of the deck, you take the other half, and each of you places his cards behind his back. The spectator is instructed to remove any 4 cards from his half and place them face down on the table as you apparently do the same thing. Actually, you remove the 4 pre-set cards and place them on the table.

If you haven't had an opportunity to pre-set the 4 queens then you must arrange to place the queens at the top of the deck without permitting your spectators to suspect that you are preparing for a trick.

Do this during the course of another trick, one that gives you the opportunity of looking at the faces of the cards.

For example, let us assume that you precede The Four Queens with a card stunt in which you apparently read the thoughts of a spectator . . . the card he has chosen. You have gained knowledge of the card, but you are creating the impression that you are trying to learn what the card is by reading the spectator's mind.

Pick the deck up, with the faces of the cards towards you, and state that by looking at the cards you will gain a stronger impression of the card the spectator is thinking of. Fan through the cards and as you mutter: "I get the impression it was a red card . . . yes, I'm quite sure . . . it was a Heart—no! a Diamond . . ." you simply move cards around in the fanned deck. But as you move them from one position to another you start setting the queens on top of the deck. Handled skillfully, your spectator will think that you are wrestling with the problem of naming his card whereas you will actually be arranging for your next stunt. Now, back to The Four Queens.

If you have placed the 4 cards in your back pocket, then you simply withdraw them as suggested above. If you haven't had an opportunity to pre-set them, then you set them on the top of the deck, as suggested above. You then hand the bottom half of the deck to the spectator, and retain the top half for yourself. Each places his half behind his back and you remove the top four cards (the queens) while the spectator removes four random cards.

Permit the spectator to give each of the packets a simple shuffle or mixing. Turn away and have the spectator place one packet on top of the other. It is unnecessary for you to know which packet is placed on top, so make a point of this as your spectator will think it is important.

Now have the spectator run through steps 1 to 5, as given in the description of the effect. At the conclusion your spectator will have 2 cards left in his hand, and packets A and B will each consist of 3 cards.

You now appear to give your spectator a free choice of the placement of the last 2 cards, but you must actually control this. The top card must be placed on packet A. The simplest way to control this is to say to the spectator: "Do you want to deal the top card onto a pile, or place it on the bottom of the cards?" If he elects to deal the top one on a pile have him do so by simply pointing to pile A. The last card, of course, is placed on B.

However, should he choose to place the top card to the bottom of the 2 he is holding permit him to do so but immediately point to pile B and indicate that the card now on top of the 2 should be dealt onto this pile. The remaining card, of course, is placed on A. In either event, your spectator will believe that he has controlled this last phase, just as he did the others, but such will not be the case.

Although the cards will seem to have been co-mingled in a hopeless fashion the two packets will actually consist of the 4 cards originally appearing in each packet! To conclude the stunt, request that the spectator place a hand on one of the packets. At this point, you have no idea as to which packet contains the 4 queens. As soon as your spectator has chosen a packet you pick up the other packet, square up the cards, and glance at the bottom card of the packet. If the bottom card is a queen you immediately say: "You have left this packet (indicating the packet *you* are holding). Isn't this an amazing coincidence!" you continue as you turn the queens packet over and display the cards.

If, when you glance at the bottom card, you note that it is an indifferent card you of course know that your spectator has selected The Four Queens. Thus, you simply toss the "indifferent" packet aside as you build up the fact that after all of the mixing and choices your spectator has made he has finally made a last choice: The cards upon which his hand now rests. Have the spectator turn over the cards his hand has been covering, and you will have a very strong climax to this stunt.

In actual performance the effect moves along at a good pace. You will find that your spectator is quite interested in his various "choices" as he will feel that you are trying to attain a certain sequence. Thus, interest will build naturally.

To understand the mechanics, I suggest you simply run through the entire explanation, using 2 packets of 4 cards. One of the packets should consist of indifferent cards, and the other the queens. You will thus be able to note the various permutations and better appreciate the "remote control" you actually retain. Do this with the cards faced upwards and the movements of the cards will be clear to you.

index

A CATALOG OF SELECTED

DOVER BOOKS

IN ALL FIELDS OF INTEREST

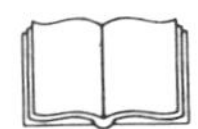